Old Tales
for a New Day

Old Tales
for a New Day

Early Answers to Life's
Eternal Questions

By
SOPHIA LYON FAHS
and
ALICE COBB

Illustrations by
GOBIN STAIR

Buffalo, New York 14215

Published by Prometheus Books
1203 Kensington Avenue
Buffalo, NY 14215

Library of Congress Catalog Number 80-84076
ISBN 0-87975-138-X

Printed in the United States of America

Table of Contents

XI. Acknowledgments

XIV. Introduction

STORIES ABOUT REACHING FOR THE GOOD

1. THE HALF-BOY OF BORNEO *(From Borneo)*   1
   If a person has both good and bad parts,
   how can he or she become one person?

2. HOW THE PEOPLE CAME   7
   TO THE MIDDLE PLACE
   (From the Tewas of North America)
   Why do people choose to live where they do,
   instead of somewhere else?

3. THE WEEPING OF THE BIRCH TREE   15
   (From Finland)
   How do we decide what we want to do
   in life?

STORIES ABOUT WHAT WE CANNOT SEE

4. THE FIG TREE AND THE SEED   20
   (From the Hindus)
   How can we know that what we cannot see
   or touch is real?

5. VOICES OF THE GREAT SPIRIT   24
   (From the Aborigines of Central Australia)
   Should we listen to voices we think we hear
   even though there seems to be nobody there?

6. THE TORTOISE AND THE TREE   29
   (From Nigeria)
   How can wisdom and knowledge, which we
   cannot see, spread all around the world?

v.

STORIES ABOUT LOVE AND LOYALTY

7. YUDISTHIRA'S FAITHFUL DOG   33
(From the Hindus)
To what extent should we be faithful to
those who need us and depend on us?

8. THE BOY WHO FOUND HIS FATHER   37
(From the Maori of New Zealand)
How can loving children stay close to
their parents, even though they are apart?

9. THE SEPARATED LOVERS *(From Korea)*   44
When, if ever, is it right to break
vows of faithfulness made between lovers?

10. THE HEALING WATERS   52
(From the Iroquois of North America)
What are some of the costs of loyalty
in marriage?

STORIES ABOUT REWARD AND PUNISHMENT

11. WATER OVER THE WORLD *(From Greece)*   58
To what extent are natural disasters
punishment for wrong-doing?

12. MAN IS PUNISHED BY THE ANIMALS   64
(From the Cherokees of North America)
To what extent is getting sick
a punishment for wrong-doing?

13. NIYAK AND THE EAGLE   71
(From the Eskimos of North America)
Why is it important to keep promises?

14. THE BOY WHO WENT TO THE SKY   81
(From the Cherokees of North America)
Why is it wrong to cheat?

STORIES ABOUT CONFLICT OVER
POWER AND POSSESSIONS

15. A DRUM TO DANCE BY   86
(From the Bakongo in Africa)
How should we decide who owns what?

16. THE CHIEF OF THE WELL *(From Haiti)*   91
To whom does the water belong?

17. NIGHT AND DAY AND THE SEASONS   96
(From the Western Mountains of Canada)
How can people reach an agreement when
their wishes are completely opposite?

STORIES ABOUT WAR AND PEACE

18. TWO SELFISH KINGS *(From the Buddhists)*   101
What is worth fighting for?

19. THE TWO SISTERS   104
(From the Capilanos of North America)
How can war be changed into peace?

20. KRISHNA, CHAMPION OF THE OPPRESSED   108
(From the Hindus)
When, if ever, is it right to go to war?

STORIES ABOUT SEEKING RICHES

21. THE KING WITH THE GOLDEN TOUCH   115
(From Greece)
What happens when one is too eager for gold?

22. THE RICH YOUNG MAN   118
(From the Early Christians)
How should riches be used?

23. THE MAGIC PILLOW *(From Ancient China)*   121
What are some of the problems
wealth may bring?

24. BLOOD OF THE POOR *(From Italy)*   125
When, if ever, should donations for
good causes be refused?

*STORIES ABOUT WHAT IS "MEN'S WORK"
AND WHAT IS "WOMEN'S WORK"*

25. WHEN FIRST MAN AND   128
FIRST WOMAN QUARRELED
(From the Navajos of North America)
What is necessary if men and women
are to get along together?

26. THE DETERMINED DAUGHTER   133
(From Ancient China)
What must women do if they are to
influence major policy decisions?

*STORIES ABOUT NATURAL POWER
AND ENERGY*

27. ZOROASTER AND THE SUN   140
(From Ancient Persia)
Why does the sun seem important enough
to be called a "god"?

28. HOW PROMETHEUS BROUGHT FIRE   145
TO THE WORLD *(From Greece)*
How did people get control of fire?

29. THE MAIZE SPIRIT   148
(From the Chippewas of North America)
What do people have to do to get food?

STORIES ABOUT HUMAN AND SPIRITUAL POWER

30. GLOOSKAP AND THE BABY   153
(From the Algonquins of North America)
What are the limits of human power?

31. THE HUNGRY MULTITUDE   156
    (From the Early Christians)
    How can a little food feed many?

32. JESUS AND THE EVIL SPIRITS   159
    (From the Early Christians)
    How can a person's spirit be healed?

33. THE BOY WHO ASKED QUESTIONS   163
    (From England)
    How can a human being discover the
    secrets of the universe?

34. THE POLLUTION DRAGON   169
    (A modern fable created by children)
    Why can people do together what
    one person cannot do alone?

STORIES ABOUT THE MEANING OF LIVING AND DYING

35. MAWU'S WAYS ARE BEST   173
    (From Benin, formerly Dohomey, in Africa)
    Why does everybody have to die?

36. THE SOLDIER DREAMS *(From the Buddhists)*   178
    When you die, is that the end of you?

37. MPOBE, THE HUNTER *(From Uganda)*   181
    Where do people go when they die?

38. THE KING'S QUESTION *(From the Buddhists)* 185
    What will we be like after we die?

39. BRAHMAN, THE UNIVERSAL BEING   189
    (From the Hindus)
    What does it mean to "live forever"?

TABLE OF CONTENTS

A WORD TO PARENTS AND TEACHERS   194
WHY A BOOK OF "OLD TALES"
FOR TODAY'S CHILDREN?

A GUIDE TO PRONUNCIATION
UNFAMILIAR NAMES AND PLACES   199

Acknowledgments

Old Tales for a New Day was born in the heart and imagination of Sophia Lyon Fahs. It grew out of her profound conviction that through their myths and legends, simple people from the earliest times can still help us today to think more deeply on basic life issues. Dr. Fahs, during her lifetime of leadership and writing on behalf of children, often turned to the campfire stories of thousands of years ago for insights to ponder with today's children. Two of her earlier books tapped these rich resources: *From Long Ago and Many Lands* and *Beginnings: Earth, Sky, Life, Death* (with Dorothy Spoerl). Both grew out of her own direct experimentation with children and later became part of the New Beacon Series in Religious Education.

The present volume was initiated in response to her wish that certain deeply challenging stories, discovered in her earliest searches, might become the core for a third published collection. In contrast to the earlier emphasis on "beginnings," this final collection, in her view, should focus on relationships between people, between people and animals and plants, and between people and their gods. When Sophia Fahs, who had been my teacher, friend, and mentor since the early forties, invited me to work with her toward the completion of such a book, I willingly agreed. To the end of her life she followed the progress of this venture with great interest and gave valuable suggestions and criticisms. After her death in 1978, I continued to discover and retell suitable stories, and prepared the companion Guidebook, *Exploring Basic Issues with Young People*, without her counsel.

Creation of *Old Tales for a New Day* was thus a shared endeavor in an unusual sense. Dr. Fahs developed over decades the book's basic philosophic and educational approach. She provided the initiative, incentive, and conceptual focus. Fourteen of the core stories are ones she herself discovered and treasured over the years. Most of these reflect her own retelling. The tasks that remained for me were the selection and adaptation of the other twenty-five stories, the initial drafting of the book's opening and closing commentaries, and the organization of the book around themes and questions. Almost to the time of her death, I consulted with her about the selections, adaptations, and commentary.

XI.

Although there have been additions and changes since then, all have been in the spirit of her original plan. It is of course impossible to ascertain in retrospect what changes she might have suggested if she had lived to review the final manuscript. In its completed form, therefore, the details of the book are primarily my responsibility.

Members of Sophia Fahs's family have also helped her dream to take shape. Her daughter, Dr. Dorothy Fahs Beck, a sociologist, has given the project long-term support as guide, organizer, facilitator, idea person, and friendly critic. Dorothy's husband, Dr. Hubert Park Beck, from his diligent library search, and his frequent challenges.

Many others have also helped to bring this book to a successful completion. Horace Peck, a literary researcher, assisted with the early searches for stories. When the manuscript was ready for review, Emily Ellis and Beulah Link, both of whom had worked with Sophia Fahs during her early experiments with children, read the manuscript and gave valuable suggestions. Emily Ellis also gave substantial help with the Guide. Emily L. Thorne, Religious Education Director for the American Ethical Union, also offered suggestions for revision of both the book and the Guide. So also did Dr. Ina Corinne Brown, well-known writer and teacher in the fields of anthropology and race relations. Marcia McBroom Landess, from her training in anthropology and her experience as Director of the School of Universal Religion at the Community Church of New York, contributed a number of suggestions for class activities and resource materials, and identified some needed revisions in the text and Glossary.

From an editorial perspective, early guidance on styling was provided by two former professors of English Composition, Sophia Crane and Mary Hill, and by Ethel Martin, who also worked with great care and persistence on manuscript preparation and typing. In the later stages, Jean Millholland, editor for both the book and the Guide, suggested further improvements and shepherded both volumes through the technicalities of the production process.

Another vital and much appreciated dimension was added by Gobin Stair, Former Director of the Beacon Press, His thirty-nine vivid and creative drawings, each with an intense focus on a single idea or feeling, add greatly to the book's impact and challenge.

Thanks are also due to those who provided encouragement, support, and guidance in times of perplexity and frustration. In this connection, special gratitude is due Dr. Ernest W. Kuebler, former Director of the Department of Religious Education for what is now the Unitarian Universalist Association; Jeannette Hopkins, publishing consultant; and Dr. Donald Harrington, Senior Minister of the Community Church of New York, and his wife, the Rev. Vilma Harrington. Through the leadership of the Harringtons, the book received a grant from the Fund for Publications in Religious Education of the Community Church of New York for partial support of publication costs.

This selective in-gathering of ancient insights for study by today's young people has been a truly cooperative enterprise. All who have joined in the task must, I am sure, consider it a rare privilege and a· sacred trust to have shared in Sophia Fahs's final volume for children. If the book proves useful in broadening horizons and deepening sympathies, then all of us can feel that this difficult mission begun years ago has at last been achieved.

Alice Cobb

Nashville, Tennessee
September 1980

Introduction

Several years ago, a group of boys and girls in a New York schoolroom played a game. They pretended they were people who lived so long ago that there were no books. In fact, they lived so long ago that there was nobody alive who could tell them anything about anything.

These boys and girls sat around on the floor in their classroom and pretended it was outdoors, at night, by a river, with a deep forest on the hillside above them. They looked up at the forest and wondered where trees came from and why they looked dead sometimes and alive other times. What made summer and winter?

They looked at the sky and wondered why sometimes it was night, with stars, and sometimes day, with sunshine. What made the sun? What does the sun do for people? They looked at the stars and wondered what stars were and where they came from and why some of them seemed to twinkle.

They looked at the river rumbling along and wondered about water. They wondered why people get thirsty and hungry.

They wondered about people and animals and how they all came to be. They wondered about how there were children and how later on the children grew up, and how people died. They wondered why people were white and brown and red and black. They wondered why people *were* at *all*!

They wondered how in the world everything got started, and why it got started in the first place.

Questions exactly like these were first asked thousands of years ago. In fact, for as long as people have lived on earth they have wondered, and they still do. They have looked for some kind of explanation about nature, sickness, death, joy, sorrow, good and evil. They have often needed reassurance because they were afraid. They have searched for ways of controlling, or for coming to terms with, the unexpected disasters of nature. They have tried to find ways of preventing evils of their own making.

From this questioning has evolved a rich accumulation of stories, handed down from generation to generation.

Some of these answers have been called myths. Myths are widely shared and accepted stories that try to explain things that puzzle us. Some of the old stories are about animals which behave like human beings and we call them "fables." Some old stories are called "legends" or "folk-tales."

Superhuman beings called "gods" have often appeared in the stories and usually people and gods have talked to each other. Sometimes, gods have been part human or humans have been part god. The same is true of animal stories. Animals have sometimes changed into people and people into animals, or people have been part animal, and people and animals have talked together. Sometimes, people and animals have been worshiped as gods and sometimes they have worshiped gods. Sometimes gods, people or animals have been deceived and made fun of by one another.

In the stories, there often have been some who were stronger, more gifted, and more powerful than others. These were the "heroes" or "heroines." Usually there have been some who did good sometimes, and bad other times. The stories were concerned with why this should be, and with how to make the best of life under all conditions.

The stories in this book come from many lands and times. They deal with some of the very questions that concern us today—questions about life and death, about good and evil, and about how to live together peacefully in one world. Philosophers, teachers, politicians, and religious leaders are still trying to solve these same old problems. Some of the explanations given today are much like the ancient ones. Even "mythmaking" itself continues today, as storytellers sometimes put their questions and answers in the form of stories with hidden meanings. The authors of this book have searched out and retold these old tales because they believe that there is a universal kinship among all people, then and now and everywhere. They believe that understanding "ancient" answers can help people work out better ways of solving today's problems.

The authors hope you will enjoy the illustrations by Gobin Stair. He has used ideas from the stories but has drawn them in such a way that you can add your own ideas as to what they might really mean to you.

Please use the Guide to Pronunciation in the back of the book. It will help you with some of the strange names of people and places.

Stories About Reaching
for the Good

1

THE HALF-BOY
OF BORNEO
(From Borneo)

If a person has both good and bad parts,
how can he or she become one person?

T HIS STORY ABOUT THE HALF-BOY of Borneo is very, very
old. It has been told by the people of the island of
Borneo in the South Pacific for hundreds of years. How
much is really true in the story and how much has been imagined as true is for readers today to think over and decide.
Here is the story:

Long, long ago on the island of Borneo, in the village of
Tambahillar, there once lived a boy who was the dread and
worry of all who came in contact with him. This was because
he was only a half-boy. Somehow, sometime, somewhere, he
had lost his good half. Now he was merely his bad half, and
the bad half was always doing bad tricks.

A woman in the village might be doing her washing in the
shallow part of the river, pounding the clothes with a stick to
get them clean. Half-Boy, who had only one hand and one
leg, would hop by on his one leg and spatter mud all over her
newly-washed clothes. Another woman might be spinning.
Half-Boy would slip up behind her, and with his one hand,
would tear the wool off the spinning wheel. A man might be
picking fruit and Half-Boy would pelt him with coconuts.

1

When Half-Boy played games with the other boys, he always seemed to find a way to spoil their fun. The women of the village called Half-Boy a pest. The boys jeered at him behind his back and threw sticks at him and the men scolded him and chased him off their fields.

As Half-Boy grew older, he became more and more annoying to the other villagers. They were almost ready to drive him out of the village, and some even wanted to kill him. There was only one young woman of the village who felt sorry for him. She believed that he might change.

One day the young woman said to him, "You are only half a person. I am sorry to say you are only the bad half. Somewhere in the world is the other half of you—the good half. If you will go away and find your other half and then come back with it and let it live with you, I will marry you!"

Half-Boy was surprised; he could hardly believe what he had heard. He even hopped away as if he had *not* heard. But later he came back to the young woman and said, "You are the first person who has ever said a kind thing about me. I will do what you say. I will start tomorrow and I will never come back until I have found my good half and am a whole boy."

Next morning, with his spear in his belt, Half-Boy started off. But where could his other half be? He had not the slightest idea. The first day he hopped along for twenty miles, almost without stopping. At evening time he came to a village deep in the jungle. The people were all sitting about a big fire when Half-Boy hopped up and asked, "Is there a half-boy here? Is there one who has only one hand and does nothing but what is kind and good?"

The villagers shook their heads. "We heard once of a person like that," one of them said, pointing to the setting sun. "He is supposed to live two days journey from here."

Next morning Half-Boy started on his second journey. This time he hopped thirty miles before he found anyone.

At last one evening he came to another village, beside a lake. Again he asked the same question, "Is there a half-boy here who has only one hand and does only good and kind things?" Everyone shook his head. They had heard of no such person.

Finally a stranger stepped up and said, "I saw a half-boy once in a village a day's journey west. But I do not know whether he is good or bad, or whether he has only one hand. I only know he was a half-boy."

With this encouragement, Half-Boy started off again on his journey. This time he hopped forty miles. It took him several days. At last at evening time he came to the ocean and a little village on the shore. Even while he was quite far off from the village, a loud cry went up from the people.

"Another half-boy!" they shouted. "Another half-boy! This one has the opposite hand missing. Where is our own half-boy? We must find him right away. He must see his brother."

While the people were still shouting and hurrying about excitedly, Half-Boy saw the other half-boy coming toward him. There could be no doubt whatever that he had at last found his other half. The two boys were the same size. They wore their hair done up the same way. One had only a right hand; the other, only a left hand. Each had a bracelet and an anklet to match the other's. The only difference anyone could see between the two was in their eyes. The eye of one was hard and cold and discouraged; the eye of the other was soft and warm and happy.

"Brother," said the bad half-boy, "I have come a long way to find you!"

"I am glad," said the other half-boy, "for I certainly would never have gone a long way to hunt you!"

"That may be true," said the bad half-boy, "but what are we going to do about it? Can we be joined together so as to make one whole boy again?"

As the two half-boys stood watching each other uneasily, the chief of the village came near. Taking each boy's one hand in his, he said, "The two of you must go off by yourselves into the bush and wrestle there. If necessary, you must wrestle for a day and a night or longer. As you wrestle, you will find yourselves growing together."

"It will be a short wrestle," said the bad half-boy. "I am strong and up to all sorts of tricks!"

"Don't be boasting," said the good half-boy. "You may find a match in me, for I too am strong. I have a spirit in me, the spirit of the sunrise, which will help me."

The bad half-boy smiled. "I have a spirit in me that is more powerful than yours," he said. "It is the spirit of the night. It can blow out the fires of the sunrise."

"Brother," said the bad half-boy, "I have come a long way to find you."

So the two half-boys went alone into the jungle. When they had found a clearing, they grabbed each other. Back and forth they swung as they wrestled. All night long they struggled. At sunrise the good half was clearly the stronger, but they still wrestled on. By sunset time, when it began to be dark, the bad half had got the upper hand. But they were not ready to stop.

All the while in the village a heavy storm raged. Lightning flashed, thunder roared, and rain flooded the land. The villagers said to one another, "Those two half-boys are not the only ones who are fighting. The stars are shooting their silver arrows at each other. Listen to the north and south winds. They are wrestling together in the palm trees."

Finally, the next morning at sunrise all was calm. The birds were singing. The wind went to sleep in the palm trees. And when the people of the village went forth from their huts, they looked out toward the jungle and behold! They saw a beautiful boy coming toward them. He held his head high and was looking in the direction of the rising sun.

"The good half must have conquered!" said the chieftain of the village. "The two half-boys are now become one person."

The people shouted for gladness. They ran to the young man and asked him to come and live with them in their village. He shook his head. "No," he said, "I shall go back to the other village where my bad half has been living. I must find the maiden who believed in me, and marry her."

After thanking the chief of the village for the help he had given, the boy with two halves said good-bye to all the villagers. He started off again alone.

After some days he finally reached his own village, but his old neighbors did not recognize him. They thought he was a stranger! Only the one young woman who had believed in Half-Boy knew him at once, and she showed the others by what signs she knew him. "Our old half-boy accepted his good half," she said, "and the two together make a real person like the rest of us."

As his old neighbors looked and listened, they began to like the new boy. But the maiden loved him, and the two were married that very day.

(This legend is found in *New Found Tales From Many Lands* by Joseph Burke Egan, published by John C. Winston Co., Philadelphia, 1929.)

2

HOW THE PEOPLE CAME TO THE MIDDLE PLACE

(From the Tewas of North America)

Why do people choose to live where they do,
instead of somewhere else?

I N THE BEGINNING THE WHOLE WORLD was dark. The
people lived underground, in the blackness. After a long
time in darkness, they began to get restless. Then Mole came
to visit them, digging his way along through the darkness
with his little paws and sharp-pointed nails. The old men of
the people asked Mole, "Is there more of a world than this,
friend?"

Mole answered, "When I go up, the world *feels* different. I
cannot see the difference because I am blind and my eyes
cannot see the daylight as yours could. Maybe if some of you
went up there and looked around, you could see whether
there is another world above or whether all there is is here
below."

"How should we travel?" the old men asked him. "How
shall we know where to go?"

"Follow along behind me," Mole replied, "I can tell you
when we come out in that different world, because I will feel
the change."

Then the people formed themselves into a line behind
Mole, and he began to dig his way upward. As Mole clawed

away the earth, the people took it from his little paw-hands and passed it back along their line, from one person to the next, to get it out of their way. That is why the tunnel that Mole dug upward for the people was closed behind them. That is why they could never find their way back to their old dark world.

When at last Mole stopped digging and the people came out in their new world they felt blinded by the light. Then the people became frightened. They hid their eyes with their hands. Some of the people said, "This is as bad as the darkness. We can see nothing here either. Let us go back!"

While the people were standing there arguing about what was best to be done, they heard a little voice of a woman speak to them.

"Be patient, my children," the small voice said, "and I will help you."

The oldest of the people asked her, "Who are you, my mother?"

Then she answered him. "Take your hands away from your eyes, but do it slowly, slowly. Then wait a minute."

Four times in all the people moved their hands. At last their eyes were opened. The people could see who was talking to them. It was the bent little old Spider Woman, the grandmother of the earth and of all living things.

Grandmother Spider sat on the ground before the people. Standing beside her were two young men, her twin grandsons, the War Twins.

Grandmother said, "These two grandsons of mine are silly. I want you people always to remember to stop whenever you are tempted to quarrel with one another. Never make yourselves weapons, because if you do you will be tempted to use them. And if you ever give in to that temptation, and do hurt one another, then you will learn what sorrow is. To be happy, you must never hurt anyone in any way."

The voice belonged to little old Spider Woman, the grandmother of the earth and of all living things.

Then Grandmother Spider pointed with her lips and chin away in the distance, and said to the oldest man, "What do you see there, my child?"

He answered her. "We see something green and growing, our Grandmother."

"That is right," said Grandmother Spider, "you see well. The name of that green growing thing is CORN, and it is food for all my people. You will have to learn to plant it and to care for it. You will have to weed it and hoe it and water it. You will have to work hard for the corn, but if you work right, with good hearts and love for each other, the corn will take care of you always."

And the oldest men of the people asked her, "Where shall we plant our cornfields, Grandmother?"

Grandmother Spider looked around her, and asked, "What do you see, my grandchildren?"

And the old men of the people answered her, "We see a red mountain in the east, Grandmother."

Grandmother Spider told them, "That is the Red Eastern Mountain. The snow on its slopes is stained red with the blood of the people who have died fighting the wild Indians who lived on the east side of the mountains. Keep away from those mountains, my children. Now the daylight is going, and soon it will be night. Look again, quickly. What do you see over there?"

"There is a white mountain to the north, Grandmother."

Spider Woman said to them, "That is Mountain Standing. If you go north of it you will be cold, my grandchildren. The corn you plant will freeze in the ground, and it will never grow for you. Now, look again. What do you see over there, grandchildren?"

And the oldest man of all the old men answered her. "We see a black mountain in the west, Grandmother."

Then Spider Woman said, "That is the Black Mountain West. Behind it is the Place Where the Sun Lies Down and Dies. If you go too far in that direction, your corn will wilt and drop in the darkness, and will never grow and ripen. Keep away from the west, my children, or you will be back in the world of night." Then she said, "Now look again. What do you see in that direction?"

And they looked again, and the youngest one of all the old men said, "We see something golden and gleaming, far away to the south of us, Grandmother. It is too far away for us to be sure what it is."

Then she answered, "That is Turtle Mountain, and when you reach it, you will know that you have reached your home."

So the old men of the people asked her, "What means that word, *turtle,* our Grandmother?"

And in a voice that was growing tired and tiny, Grandmother Spider answered them, "When you find the signs of your two friends again—when you find Mole again and me again—then you will have found the turtle and his mountain that he carries on his back." Grandmother Spider's voice faded as the daylight faded. She and her twin grandsons were gone.

The people huddled together all that long night—the first night they had ever known. They looked above them and saw the stars—white against the blackness, like sparks that had scattered off the sun. They watched as the stars walked across the sky.

When morning came, the stars faded and vanished. The people, standing there in full daylight, began to quarrel. Some wanted to go one way, some another. They all wanted to go straight to the mountains they could see most clearly, in the east, in spite of Grandmother Spider's warning. Those mountains looked closer to them than the Turtle Mountain she had told them was to be their home.

At last the people decided to travel to the Red Mountain of the East. There the Comanches surprised them, and before the people could defend themselves, many of them were killed. The white snow on the mountain was dyed red with their blood.

Again the people quarreled among themselves, for some of them wanted to go south and others north. Some of these last people picked up sharp-pointed stones, like knives and spearheads, and hit their brothers with them. Then they ran away, to the north. When they came to the cold slope of the mountain a white bear came down its side, and breathed its cold breath on them. Some of the people fell down dead. Those who were alive ran away, as fast as they could, sorrowing. The bear went back up the mountain, and on up into the sky. You can see him there in winter, early in the night.

Again the people began to quarrel among themselves about which way they should go. Some made themselves spears and became spear throwers. They hurled the spears at their brothers and pierced them. And the men who were pierced fell down and died.

The others, weeping, ran away to the west, toward the Black Mountain, guarded by the War Twins. The twins shook their own weapons at the people, and threatened them, saying "Go away, you foolish people, for this is the Place Where the Sun Lies Down and Dies. This is where every living thing must die. You cannot stay here and live."

Then the War Twins turned their backs, and went back up the Black Mountain, into the sky. You can see them there in the springtime, about the middle of the night.

So the people turned sorrowfully away from the laughing War Twins in the western sky and started traveling back. Their feet were tired; their sandals were worn out. They traveled back over the black lava beds, and the knife-edged stones cut their feet. The people left a trail of bloody footprints behind them. You can see the red marks on the sharp black lava today.

Then the weary people hunted for the place where they had come out. They looked for their grandmother, but she was not there. When night came, they looked into the sky above their heads, and learned why they could not find her. Grandmother Spider sat there in her star web, shaking her head and crying little star tears because her people were so foolish. Some of the people cried, too. They ran away, up into the sky, to join their grandmother. The white road along which they ran is the Milky Way.

Now there were only two of all the people left, a man and a woman. They were very tired. Because there was nowhere else left for them to go, they turned and journeyed south. Their road was hard. They traveled through the desert, and it was dusty and sandy. At last the woman stopped and looked around her.

"There are green trees over there to our right," she said.

The man looked at the dry world all around them, and he replied, "Let us go over there and look at them. At least we can sit down in the shade and be cool."

So they crossed the heavy sand and came to the line of green trees. There was a line of blue water, shining beyond the trees. It was the Rio Grande.

The woman said to her husband, "Indeed, this is a very beautiful place. Let us sit down here and rest, for the world feels as if it would be good to us."

After the man had rested a while and felt stronger, he looked around him. He said to the woman, "Look! There is a golden mountain over there, shining and gleaming, across the valley to the south. I wonder what it is?"

The woman warned him, "Keep away from it. Stay away from it forever. You know what happened to our people who went up into the other mountains."

So the man sat still on the river bank beside her, but he sat facing the golden mountain.

Presently the woman looked down at the sand beside her.

"Look!" she said to her husband. "Something is crawling along the sand. I wonder what that little thing is, moving so slowly, slowly?"

Then the man, in his turn, warned her. "Leave it alone. You know what happened to our people who went near the dangerous animal, on the Mountains of the North."

The woman obeyed her husband, and did not touch the little crawling thing as it moved slowly along the sand.

The man said to his wife, "Look what a strange track this thing leaves in the sand. We have seen tracks like that before somewhere, haven't we? They look like the mole's tracks, don't they?"

The woman studied the little animal, and then said "Look!

Its back is as hard as stone, but it has a design carved and painted on it. Look! That design is Grandmother Spider's web!"

Together the man and the woman watched the little crawling thing. Together they said to each other. "Look! It is shaped like the Shining Golden Mountain!"

They looked again at the far away golden gleam of the mountain. They looked down again at the little turtle, crawling along the sand. They looked at each other and they smiled. They had found their friends Mole and Spider again, and their friend had shown the man and woman their home, as Grandmother Spider had promised he would.

(This story came from *American Indian Mythology,* by Alice Marriott and Carol Rachlin, published by Thomas Y. Crowell Company, New York, 1968. Copyright © 1968 by Alice Marriott and Carol K. Rachlin. Reprinted by permission of Harper & Row, Publishers, Inc.)

3
THE WEEPING OF
THE BIRCH TREE
(From Finland)

How do we decide what we want
to do in life?

V AINAMOINEN WAS AN OLD MAN when this story happened. He had seen many summers and winters in the cold northland of Finland. Perhaps his heart had grown large and warm with the years. Perhaps that was why he could hear and understand the birch tree when she wept in the forest.

"Why are you so sad?" he asked her. "you are so beautiful in your silver robe. You should be proud and merry!"

The birch tree trembled and then spoke to the old man about her trouble. "I weep because I am so small," she confessed. "I am small and weak and lonely here in the forest with all these mighty pines and hemlocks. They wait for the summer with pleasure, but I wait only with pain and dread."

"Pain?" he asked in wonder. "Dread?"

She trembled again. "The children will come and peel my bark for making little baskets," she exclaimed. "And the young girls will bind my twigs into stupid brooms and brushes for sweeping. Strong men will chop my limbs into chips for burning."

"These are all useful things," Vainamoinen observed.

"But small and trifling!" she exclaimed. "Others make ships and houses. My gifts are so little. I would like to bring

15

The birch tree trembled and then spoke to the old man...

pleasure in great quantities to many people!"

Vainamoinen's great warm heart was touched and at once he answered her with welcome words. "Your gifts are useful to men," he assured her, "but I can understand how you want to bring joy and I believe I can turn your grief into joy. So don't weep any more! Soon you will be singing!"

At once he began cutting the birch tree and carving the slim white trunk into a tall harp. When that was done he looked about and asked himself, "Where can I get strings for this harp? Five strings I need to make the birch tree sing!"

Wondering in this way, he walked about in the forest and along the heath. At last he came upon a lovely young girl who sat alone, singing softly to herself. She was singing a love song, Vainamoinen knew.

He came up softly, in order not to frighten her, and spoke to her. "O lovely maiden," he said, "please give me some of your hair."

The girl was startled but not frightened.

"It is for my harp," he explained. "It is to help the birch tree harp to sing."

She gave him the hairs willingly and he fastened them one by one to the harp. At last the task was finished. The old man could hardly wait to try playing on his creation. But he wanted to make the trial just right. So he first selected a rock for his seat, exactly the right height. He sat down with the tall harp beside him. Then he took it gently in his hands, put the strings in order, and made the first soft strokes across them with his fingers.

And what melodious music! The birchwood seemed to ring; the hair of the maiden seemed to rejoice.

> Mountains shook and plains resounded,
> All the rocky hills resounded,
> In the waves the stones were rocking,
> In the water moved the gravel,
> And the pine trees were rejoicing,
> On the heath the stumps were skipping.

Boys and girls and men and women from the village heard the music and came flocking toward the harp. The young women laughed; the mothers were joyful.

The men came holding their caps in their hands. The old women came holding their hands to their sides. The young women's eyes shed tear drops of happiness they could not understand. The boys knelt before them and they danced and sang all together. Never before had they heard such beautiful music.

The music went farther and farther. In six villages they heard it. Every creature hurried forth from house and work to listen and to dance.

All the wild beasts of the forest came and they stood upright on their claws to listen. All the birds flying in the air came to perch on the branches of nearby trees. All the fish swimming in the rivers hastened to the shore. Even the worms in the earth came creeping up above the ground to listen to the music of the birch tree.

But that was not all. Even the walls and ceilings of the houses resounded, the doors creaked, the windows rejoiced, and the hearthstones moved. Out in the woods all the pine-woods and firwoods bowed down before the harp. The pine cones rolled about on the ground scattering the needles. The leaves called gaily across the heath. The flowers breathed fragrance toward the music; and the young shoots bowed.

"Happy birch tree!" they sang with the music. "All the world is merry with your singing!"

(From: *Kalevala: The Land of the Heroes,* translated by W.F. Kirby and published by Aldine Press, Letchworth, Herts, England, 1907.)

Stories About What
We Cannot See

4

THE FIG TREE AND THE SEED
(From the Hindus)

How can we know that what we cannot
see or touch is real?

ONCE UPON A TIME there was a boy in India named
Svetakatu, who was the son of a priest. When Svetakatu was very young his father said to him, "Svetakatu, my
son, it is time you went somewhere to study about God.
There is no one in our family who has not studied about
God. It is time now for you, Svetakatu, my son, to begin
your study also."

So Svetakatu became a pupil of a famous wise teacher. He
learned to read many long books about the world and about
God. He could repeat word for word many pages from the
great books. He knew by heart many long prayers and he
could sing and play songs without end. He knew all the
things that should be done and should not be done at the
celebrations of the holy days.

At last, very proud of all his knowledge, Svetakatu went
back home, thinking that he knew much more than his
father. With great happiness the father welcomed his son,
but as they visited again together, the father saw that Svetakatu was conceited and thought too highly of himself. So
one day he took a walk with his son and the two sat down
together on some rocks in the midst of a grove of fig trees. A
short distance away, a lovely river flowed past them.

20

Then the father said to Svetakatu, "My son, since now you think you have learned so much, you are proud and conceited. I want to ask you a question. Have you learned how that which has not been heard can be heard? Or have you learned how that which has not been thought of can be thought of? Have you learned how that which has not been understood can be understood?"

Svetakatu replied, "No, father; teach me that teaching."

So the father said, "Bring me a fig from that fig tree."

So the son picked a fig from the tree and brought it to his father. "Here it is, sir," he said.

"Cut it open," said his father.

"I have cut it open," said the son.

"What do you see there?" asked the father.

"Oh, some small seeds, sir."

"Cut open one of the seeds," said the father.

"I have cut one open, sir."

"What do you see there?" asked the father.

"Nothing at all, sir," replied the son.

"Now Svetakatu, my son, you know that there must be something there. You know that that great fig tree grew from just such a small seed."

"Yes, father, I know."

"Then did the tree grow from something you cannot see?" asked the father.

"It must be," said Svetakatu.

"You mean, Svetakatu, that what is alive, what made the tree to grow, you cannot see?" asked the father.

"It must be so," said the son.

"Then you should know also, Svetakatu, my son, that not just in the fig seed, but everywhere there is that which is alive which no man can see. The fig tree could never have grown without that in the seed which is invisible. So nothing in the world could have been without that invisible and living part from which it came. Svetakatu, my son, the invisible everywhere in the world is the spirit in the world. It is God. God gave you life. God *is* your life."

Then Svetakatu no longer felt proud and conceited. He wished to know how to ask his father more questions.

"Oh, father," he begged, "make me understand even more."

"It shall be so, my son," said the father. "You shall learn even more."

He took a lump of salt in his hand and gave it to Svetakatu, saying, "Go, place this salt in a pan of water."

But Svetakatu answered, "Father, I do not see it any more."

Svetakatu did as his father asked him to do.

After a while the father said, "That lump of salt I handed you—please bring it back to me."

But Svetakatu answered, "Father, I do not see it any more."

Then the father said, "Put your mouth down into the end of the pan and taste the water. Tell me, how is it there?"

Svetakatu put his mouth down into the water. "The water tastes salty," he said.

"Then take a sip at the further end of the pan, my son. How is it there?"

"It is salty there also."

"You say it is salty, my son, and yet you say you cannot see any salt?"

"No, sir, I can see none at all."

"My son," said the father, "even though your eyes do not see any salt, you have found that what was before just a small lump of salt is now in the end of the pan of water. It is also in the middle, and it is even at the farther end. There is salt everywhere in the water. Now, Svetakatu, my son, you should know also that, although your eyes do not help you to see God, yet there are other ways by which you can know God is everywhere, here, there, far off. Like the salt hidden in the water, so is God hidden in all the world. God is spirit. God is all that which is really, really true. God is you, my son."

Then Svetakatu said, "Father, make me to understand even more."

"It shall be so, my son," said the father. "You shall learn more some other time."

(The Fig Tree and The Seed is adapted from two stories from the Upanishads "The Fig Tree" and "The Lump of Salt" translated orally for the senior author by the late Dr. Robert E. Hume from and Sanskrit. The story is also included in Dr. Hume's scholarly book *The Thirteen Principal Upanishads, Translated from the Sanskrit*. Oxford University Press, 1921.)

5

VOICES OF THE GREAT SPIRIT

(From the Aborigines of Central Australia)

Should we listen to voices we think we hear even though there seems to be nobody there?

THIS STORY IS PROBABLY several thousands of years old. It was first told by people who could neither read nor write, who had not learned how to make gardens or grow crops. A very simple people they were, who lived in huts made of branches of trees, who moved often from place to place in order to hunt wild animals and to hunt for wild berries and fruits to eat. They were the first hunters to find their way to the great continent of Australia. They have been called "black fellows" by the white folks who came later to live on that continent. A few of their descendants still live in the deserts of Central Australia. Now the story:

In that far away time it is said that dreams used to come true and that the Great Spirit in the sky used to talk directly to the people of the earth every day. Early each morning just as the sun was rising above the hills, the people of the earth used to gather together under a big Gum Tree to listen to what the Great Spirit would say. They could hear his voice, but no one ever saw him. In this way, the people of the earth learned about many things they could not understand, that

24

were hidden from their eyes. The Great Voice encouraged them to try to learn. And so it was for many years.

At last the people of the earth grew tired of rising so early in the morning to listen to the Great Spirit.

"I'm tired of trying to listen to a voice when I cannot see who is speaking," someone said, and then another and another complained. "It isn't worth the trouble. Let's enjoy ourselves and eat and sleep and dance as much as we please," they said.

The Great Spirit was much disappointed with the people of the earth; yet he was not willing to desert them entirely. He decided, instead, to send a special messenger to live on the earth with them—a very good man who could teach them and help them. Nurunderi was his name.

So, one day Nurunderi appeared among the earth people. When they saw him, they liked him. They welcomed him as a friend. They were helped by the things he taught them.

For a while they were quite content. They hunted the wild animals. They gathered fruits and berries. They made love; they had their exciting dances; babies were born and old people died.

But there were some among them who never forgot those early mornings they had spent under the big Gum Tree. They remembered when they could hear the Great Voice coming down from the everywhere above. They began to feel lonesome in the great big world. There was so much they wanted to know. They were sad sometimes and longed to be comforted.

Finally, they went to find Nurunderi and began to beg him. "You still rise early every morning and listen to the Great Spirit," they said. "Please ask him to speak to us again."

"No," said Nurunderi. "I'm sorry, but I cannot help you. The Great Spirit has said he will never speak again so that men can hear him."

This made the people of the earth feel very sad. Why had they ever let themselves stop listening to the voice of the Great Spirit? They began to feel lonesome in the great world with no one but themselves to talk with. They went to the places where their dead had been buried. They called to their spirits. "Speak to us!" they begged. But the spirits of their dead were silent.

The people of the earth cried and cried, but no word came back to answer. Finally, they returned to Nurunderi and begged him once more to speak for them to the Great Spirit. At last, Nurunderi announced that he had been given a message for them by the Great Spirit.

"He says for all of you to gather once more under the great Gum Tree," said Nurunderi. "But come this time when it is dark, in the middle of the night. He says he will not speak to you again, but he will give you a sign."

So the people of the earth did as Nurunderi told them. In the middle of the night when all was dark, they gathered once more under the Big Gum Tree. There they sat quietly in the dark, each one wondering what was going to happen.

As time passed, they began to be afraid. They called to the stars above them. The white Milky Way stretched across the sky like a ring of soft starlit snow folded above them. "The Man in the Milky Way is watching us," they thought. They cried out to him in their fear. "Wyunduro, we beg of you to ask the Great Spirit to speak to us again."

Suddenly, a very bright streak of fire shot down from the sky on to the top of the Gum Tree. It went right on down into its trunk, splitting the tree wide open. Then, just as quickly as it had split the tree, the streak of fire flashed up into the sky and the tree closed itself up as if nothing had happened.

Immediately Wyunduro, the Man of the Milky Way, spoke. "Did you see that tongue of fire go right into the tree?" he asked them.

"Yes, we saw, and we are frightened," they said. "We do not understand what it means."

"Take this as a sign," said the voice that came down from the Milky Way. "Know that the tongue of the Great Spirit is now in everything around you. The voice of the Great Spirit will be in every sound you hear. The Great Spirit is everywhere and hides in everything. Listen! The Great Spirit will speak, but in different ways. Try to understand!"

Then all was quiet. The people of the earth sat listening. The wind blew through the branches of the Gum Tree. The

...Great Spirit still speaks in the lightning and in the sound of the wind. ...

people of the earth wondered. They tried to understand.

Even today some of the people who live in the wild country of Central Australia may tell you that the Tongue of the Great Spirit still speaks in the lightning and in the sound of the wind blowing through the trees. It speaks in the thunder and in the song of the birds. It speaks in the soft bubbling of springs and in the roar of great rivers. The little spirits are hidden everywhere — in trees, in flowers, in birds, in fish — in everything that men of the earth can see and hear and smell and feel.

The people say, "Try to talk to the Great Spirit. You will not hear the answer, but at least know that one of the little spirits is there!"

(This story has been adapted from *Myths and Legends of the Australian Aborigines* by Wm. Ramsey Smith, London: Harrup, 1930.) Reprint permission granted by George G. Harrap & Co., Ltd., London.

6
THE TORTOISE AND THE TREE
(From Nigeria)

How can wisdom and knowledge, which we cannot see, spread all around the world?

M R. TORTOISE WAS THE CLEVEREST and most cunning animal. Because of this, he was given a praise title on the talking drum that went like this:

> Son of Alika,
> The fearsome one,
> He who dug in the earth
> And struck a water fountain.

Mr. Tortoise took many other praise titles as well. He was boastful before the world, but in private he worried much about losing his wisdom. He feared that his neighbors were jealous and might try to steal part or all of his cunning. He decided to put all his bits of knowledge, tricks, and ideas into a gourd with a long slender neck and a big round bowl. He then corked it tightly shut. He tied a tough string to the neck of the gourd and passed it around his own neck so that the gourd hung down on his chest. Mr. Tortoise found the tallest tree in the middle of the forest. In the dead of night, he proceeded to climb to the top. But since the gourd hung down in front of him, he could not get a good grip on the trunk of the tree. He fell down with each attempt he made. All night long he toiled without success.

Mr. Duiker, a small African antelope, came past early in the morning. "Good morning, Mr. Tortoise," said he. "Why are you sweating so early this morning?"

"Hello, Mr. Duiker," answered the Tortoise. "Thank you for asking. I have all that is precious to me tucked inside this gourd. I plan to hang it up on top of this tree. My problem is how to get it there."

"That is easy," said Mr. Duiker. "All you need to do is place the gourd behind instead of in front of you and climb. Then you can get a firm grip on the trunk of the tree with no trouble. Once you get to the top, you can turn the gourd around and fasten it to a branch."

Mr. Tortoise did as he was advised and soon reached the top of the tree. Once there, however, he realized that he was not so clever as he had thought. Even the humble Mr. Duiker was able to solve a problem that he, Mr. Tortoise, could not

But it is also why no one person has been able to learn all there is to know.

tackle! He felt so disgusted with himself that he let the gourd drop to the ground, where it broke into a thousand pieces.

And that is how wisdom and knowledge were scattered all over the universe and why every man, woman, boy, and girl is able to pick up a little bit of it for himself. But it is also why no one person has ever been able to learn all there is to know.

(This story was taken from the *UNICEF Book of Children's Legends,* Stackpole Books, Harrisburg, Pa., 1970. By permission of the author, William I. Kaufman, 16812 Charmel Lane, Pacific Palisades, CA. 90272.)

Stories About Love
and Loyalty

7

YUDISTHIRA'S FAITHFUL DOG

(From the Hindus)

To what extent should we be faithful to
those who need us and depend on us?

GOOD KING YUDISTHIRA HAD RULED over the Pandava
people for many years and had led them in a successful, but very long war against giant forces of evil. At the end
of his labors, Yudisthira felt that he had had enough years
on earth and it was time to go on to the kingdom of the
Immortals. When all his plans were made, he set out for the
high Mt. Meru to go from there to the Celestial City. His
beautiful wife, Drapaudi, went with him and also his four
brothers. Very soon, they were joined by a dog which followed quietly behind him.

But the journey to the mountain was a long and sorrowful
one. Yudisthira's four brothers died one by one along the
way, and after that his wife, the beautiful Drapaudi. The
King was all alone then, except for the dog, which continued
to follow him faithfully up and up the steep, long road to the
Celestial City.

At last the two, weak and exhausted, stopped before the
gates of Heaven. Yudisthira bowed humbly there as he asked
to be admitted.

Sky and earth were filled with a loud noise as the God
Indrus, God of a Thousand Eyes, arrived to meet and welcome the King to Paradise. But Yudisthira was not quite

ready.

"Without my brothers and my beloved wife, my innocent Drapaudi, I do not wish to enter heaven, O Lord of all the deities," he said.

"Have no fear," Indus answered. "You shall meet them all in heaven. They came before you and are already there!"

But Yudisthira had yet another request to make.

"This dog has come all the way with me. He is devoted to me. Surely for his faithfulness I cannot leave him outside! And besides, my heart is full of love for him!"

Indus shook his great head and the earth quaked.

"You yourself may have immortality," he said, "and riches and success and all the joys of heaven. You have won these by making this hard journey. But you cannot bring a dog into heaven. Cast off the dog, Yudisthira! It is no sin!"

"But where would he go?" demanded the king. "And who would go with him? He has given up all the pleasures of earth to be my companion. I cannot desert him now."

The god was irritated at this.

"You must be pure to enter Paradise," he said firmly. "Just to *touch* a dog will take away all the merits of prayer. Consider what you are doing, Yudisthira. Let the dog go!"

But Yudisthira insisted. "O God of a Thousand Eyes, it is difficult for a person who has always tried to be righteous to do something that he knows is *un*righteous — even in order to get into heaven. I do not wish immortality if it means casting off one that is devoted to me."

Indus urged him once more.

"You left on the road behind you your four brothers and your wife. Why can't you also leave the dog?"

But Yudisthira said, "I abandoned those only because they had died already and I could no longer help them nor bring them back to life. As long as they lived I did not leave them."

"You are willing to abandon heaven, then, for this dog's sake?" the god asked him.

This dog has come all the way with me.

"Great God of all Gods," Yudisthira replied, "I have steadily kept this vow—that I will never desert: one that is frightened and seeks my protection, one that is afflicted and destitute, or one that is too weak to protect himself and desires to live. Now I add a fourth. I have promised never to forsake one that is devoted to me. I will not abandon my friend."

Yudisthira reached down to touch the dog and was about to turn sadly away from heaven when suddenly before his very eyes a wonder happened. The faithful dog was changed into Dharma, the God of Righteousness and Justice.

Indus said, "You are a good man, King Yudisthira. You have shown faithfulness to the faithful and compassion for all creatures. You have done this by renouncing the very gods themselves instead of renouncing this humble dog that was your companion. You shall be honored in heaven, O King Yudisthira, for there is no act which is valued more highly and rewarded more richly than compassion for the humble."

So Yudisthira entered the Celestial City with the God of Righteousness beside him. He was reunited there with his brothers and his beloved wife to enjoy eternal happiness.

(From *The Mahabharata,* translated into English prose by Krishna-Dwaipayana Vyasa. This translation published by Sundari Bala Roy, Bharata Press, Calcutta. No. 1, Raja Gooroo Dasa St., 1896.)

8

THE BOY
WHO FOUND
HIS FATHER

(From the Maori of New Zealand)

How can loving children stay close to
their parents even though they are apart?

M AUI WAS A GREAT HERO of the Maori people. This
story is told all over the South Sea islands.

When Maui was a young boy he lived with his mother and
his brothers. Maui couldn't even remember his father. He
was puzzled too about his mother. She always went away
early in the morning and never came back until night. He
was left with his older brothers, but he learned as they grew
older that the brothers were not very loving and kind. When
he tried to make them laugh (for he was a good-humored
boy), they were angry and hit him and told him to go away.
"Nobody wants you here," they said. "You are a little
nuisance."

Then Maui would go off into the forest and play with the
birds which loved him. He loved them too and talked with
them. He was really very happy as he grew older, even
though he was often lonely.

There was only one thing that made Maui unhappy. He
did wish that he could see his father. No one would tell him
anything about his father. Sometimes he wondered if he really

had one.

Of course, too, there was the mystery about his mother which puzzled him more and more as he grew to young manhood. He never saw her in the daytime at all. At night, when everyone went into the *whare* (the shelter in which they slept), his mother was there. He slept beside her on a mat on the floor. But when he woke up in the morning his mother had gone. Her sleeping mat was always rolled up neatly by his. He never saw her during the day.

"Where does mother go in the daytime?" he sometimes asked his brothers.

"How should we know?" they said.

"Because you have known her longer than I have," Maui said.

The brothers turned away impatiently. "She may go north, or south, or east, or west," they said. "We don't know and we don't care. Find out for yourself if you want to know."

"Yes, that's just what I will do," Maui said to himself. "They don't care because they don't love her, but I love my mother, and I want to know what happens to her. If I could know where she goes in the daytime, perhaps I would be able to find my father also!"

The next night Maui lay awake when the fire died down in the sleeping house. He heard his mother breathing quietly and knew that she was asleep. Then he got up and crept to her side. He picked up her beautiful apron and cloak and hid them under his sleeping mat. Going softly on tiptoe, he went to the window and to the door and blocked up the cracks where the light would creep in when morning would come.

"Perhaps she won't know it's morning if the light doesn't come in," he said to himself. "Maybe she'll keep on sleeping!"

Maui hoped that he would wake up early himself, but he was a sound sleeper. When he finally did wake up it was the light coming in through the open door that roused him. His mother had already gone!

He jumped up and ran to the door just in time to see her disappearing through the village. He ran out behind too late to overtake her before she went out through a gate of the fence of the village. Hiding behind the great post of the gateway, he saw her stoop and pull up a tussock of grass with a lump of earth clinging to it. Underneath there must be a hole, he thought, because his mother jumped down into it and pulled the clod on top of her.

Maui ran back to the *whare,* where his brothers, now awake, had gathered around the window wondering who had stuffed grass into the cracks.

"I have seen where our mother goes in the daytime," he shouted excitedly. "She has gone down into a hole in the ground!"

"Silly!" his eldest brother cried. "That's just one of the ways into the Underworld, where men and women live far underground. What does it matter where she goes as long as she leaves us plenty to eat!"

"But I want to be with her," Maui said. "If she is in the Underworld, perhaps she can show us where our father is. Perhaps she is with him now! Let's follow her and see!"

The brothers looked at Maui scornfully. "What do we care where she is?" one of them said. "Great Heaven is our father and the Earth is our mother. If our true mother leaves us, she surely cannot love us!"

"But I love *her!*" Maui said. "She is my mother and I believe she loves us. She brings us food and stays with us at night. I'm going to find her!"

He went to his sleeping mat and drew out his mother's clothes, which he had hidden during the night. He tied the apron around his waist and put the feathered cloak around his shoulders. Then he said some magic words which he had once heard, and he began to grow smaller. He slipped his arms inside the cloak which covered him right up to the chin.

His nose grew longer until it looked like a beak.

Then he began to change in shape. His nose grew longer until it looked like a beak. His eyes became small and round.

His mouth disappeared. The only other part of him which showed was his feet and, while his brothers watched in amazement, Maui's feet turned into claws. The apron glowed with green and purple in the sunlight, and the beautiful white feathers of the cloak shone like the plumage of a wood-pigeon.

"Look!" cried the eldest brother. "Maui has turned into a kereru bird."

It was true. By magic spells and because of the love he had for his mother, Maui had changed himself into a forest bird. He spread his white wings and jumped into the air. He fluttered lightly to the ground. He jumped again and, with strong wings beating, he soared into the air over his brothers' heads. He flew over the tall fence, and glided into the long grass. He lifted the tuft of grass with his beak and plunged into the hole underneath.

It was dark when the earth settled over his head, but soon Maui's eyes became used to the gloom. He saw that he was in a narrow cave which sloped steeply downwards. Maui flew down it, through the winding passage that led to the Underworld. After he had flown for a long time, he came to a strange and beautiful country. There was no sun and there were no clouds and the air was still. Trees grew there, tall and leafy, but no wind stirred their branches. Far above was a sky of polished rock, and the only thing that moved was a stream which flowed beneath the trees.

Maui flew up, perched himself on a branch of a karaka tree and looked around him. For a time everything was still. Then he saw some men and women in the distance. As they came closer, Maui saw that his mother was among them. By her side was a tall man who must surely be his father. They came closer until finally they were right under his tree. Then they sat down on the ground. Maui bent his neck and picked a berry from a twig. He dropped it so that it fell on his father's head.

"That berry must have been dropped by a bird," said Maui's mother.

"No," said his father. "It was a ripe berry and its time for falling had come."

Then Maui picked up a whole cluster of the berries. He jerked them with his beak so that they scattered as they fell and hit both his mother and his father. This time they knew that the berries must have been thrown at them on purpose, so they sprang to their feet. Some other people nearby hurried up to see what was happening.

Everyone could see Maui now. They wondered about his white feathers and shining breast. They were so much brighter than the plumage of the birds of that land.

"Look!" someone shouted. "This is not a bird of the Underworld. It has come from the place where the sun shines." Some of the men threw stones at the strange bird and tried to knock him off his perch. But Maui dodged from side to side so that none of the stones hit him.

Then Maui's own father picked up a stone and threw it. Maui saw it coming and at once tumbled off his perch and fluttered to the ground. As he fell he grew bigger and less like a bird. Once again he became, in a few minutes, a tall and handsome young boy. His mother's beautiful cloak was hanging from his shoulders and the apron was around his waist.

Taranga, his mother, knew him at once and threw her arms around her young son.

"This is our youngest child," she said to her husband. "It is Maui, and he loves us more than any of the other children. He has come bravely into the Underworld to find us." Then she turned to Maui. "This is your own father, Maui! He loves you too," she said.

Maui's father put his hand on his son's shoulder. "I can see you are brave," he said, "and the son of a chief. Some day you will be a great chief yourself, and I shall be proud of you. Greetings, my son!"

"Maui is the child that came by wind and wave," Taranga told her husband. "He will bring joy and sorrow into the world. He will tie up the sun and bring many good things to his people. Some day he will fight the terrible goddess of death, and perhaps he will conquer her!"

But Maui's mother spoke to his father in magic words. Maui himself did not know any of these things. Even if he had he would not have cared, for now he had found his mother and father.

Even Maui's friends, the birds of the forest, were happy because of this. To show that they loved him, the wood pigeons wore the glowing colors of his mother's apron upon their snow-white breasts.

(This story comes from *Maori Tales of Long Ago,* by Alexander W. Reed, published by A. H. and A. W. Reed, Wellington, New Zealand, 1957.) Adapted with permission of A.H. and A.W. Reed, Wellington, New Zealand.

9
THE SEPARATED LOVERS
(From Korea)

When, if ever, is it right to break vows
of faithfulness made between lovers?

Yɪ Dᴏʀʏᴜɴɢ ᴡᴀs ᴛʜᴇ sᴏɴ of a Magistrate in old Korea.
He was a rich and handsome young man, and a student.

One beautiful morning, Yi Doryung called his servant and
asked to be guided to a place where he might see wild
flowers. So the servant led his young master to a summer
pavilion near a bridge where the stream was as beautiful as
the Milky Way in the sky.

Gazing at the distant mountains, Yi Doryung caught sight
of a young maiden, sitting in a swing under the branches of a
great tree. According to the custom of the time, she was
attended and protected by a maid whose name was "Red
Fragrance."

Approaching, Yi Doryung asked the maid about her mis-
tress and learned that her name was Choonhyang, which
means "Spring Fragrance."

"It would be difficult for you to meet Choonhyang
because she is not only beautiful, but very good, and she will
not speak to strangers," the servant said.

Just then the girl, frightened at being watched, jumped
down from her swing, arranged her dress neatly, and ran
toward her house. Stopping for a second under a peach tree
at her garden gate, she plucked a blossom and kissed it! Her

Stopping for a second under a peach tree at her garden gate, she plucked a blossom and kissed it!

lips and cheeks were redder than the bloom. Then she was gone!

Yi Doryung knew that the beautiful girl was sending him a message! He returned to his home as if in a dream. He went at once to his room, opened a book and tried to read. But the words blurred before his eyes, so that every word looked like "Spring" and "Fragrance"! Choonhyang, Choonhyang, Choonhyang!

Calling his servant, Yi Doryung declared, "I must see Choonhyang—now! At once. Take me to her home!"

Accordingly, Yi Doryung put on his finest clothes and they went together that very afternoon to the home of the beautiful girl. When they stopped under a peach tree in the garden, Choonhyang's mother saw them and came out to ask what they wanted. Yi Doryung told her immediately that he had come to ask for the hand of her daughter. The old woman thought that her dream of a good marriage for her daughter had come true and consented gladly. But there was one problem.

"You are a nobleman's son," she reminded him. "Choonhyang is a daughter of humble birth."

Yi Doryung knew that according to the law a marriage between an aristocrat and a "commoner" was out of the question. But that made no difference. He was determined to marry the beautiful Choonhyang!

"Will you accept a pledge of my faithfulness?" he asked.

"Yes," said the mother, "if you will give a pledge not ever to desert my daughter, I shall be contented."

Seizing a pen, Yi Doryung set down the following lines:

> The blue sea may become a mulberry field,
> The mulberry field may become the blue sea,
> But my heart for Choonhyang shall never change,
> Heaven and earth and all the gods are witnesses.

Three days later, a letter came from the King, announcing that the Magistrate, Yi Doryung's father, was recalled to the capital city, Seoul. Of course, that meant that Yi Doryung had to go, too.

He went that evening to tell Choonhyang what had happened and to take tender leave of her. She saw him off at the Magpie Bridge where they had first met.

"Since there is no help for it, let us embrace and part," said Choonhyang. "But here is my ring. This is my token of love for you. Keep it until we meet again. Go in peace, but do not forget me. I shall remain faithful to you, and wait here until you come to take me away to Seoul."

Soon after that, Yi Doryung and his father left that town and a new magistrate came to take office. Having already heard of the beauty of Choonhyang, the man wanted to take her for himself.

"Show me this pretty girl!" he ordered. "Bring her here to me."

"That is difficult, sir," replied the retainer, who was a friend of Choonhyang's family. "She is betrothed to Yi Doryung, the son of the former Magistrate."

The new official, in anger, ordered the girl to be brought to him at once. When she stood before him, he looked at her attentively.

"I have heard about you," he said, "and today I see that you are indeed a very pretty girl. I want you to belong to me. You will be rich and favored."

After a long silence, Choonhyang answered him.

"Sir," she said, "I have vowed to be faithful to Yi Doryung. As for you, the King has sent you here to take care of the people. You had better fulfill your duties and apply justice to the poor."

The rage of the new Magistrate knew no bounds! That he should be so insulted by a mere "commoner"! And a woman! He ordered Choonhyang to be imprisoned at once.

Meanwhile, Yi Doryung had arrived in Seoul, where he passed his examinations with highest distinction. As the days and weeks went by, the King liked him and admired his talents more and more. He was finally appointed His Majesty's Royal Envoy. Thus, Yi Doryung and all his attendants, disguised as beggars, were sent to travel around the country to inquire about the needs of the people. After some weeks, they arrived at the small farming village where Choonhyang lived. They found the people planting rice.

Approaching one of them, Yi Doryung said, "I have heard that the new Magistrate here has married the maid Choonhyang and that they now live together happily. Is this true?"

"How dare you speak like that?" the peasant exclaimed. "Choonhyang is faithful, true and pure, and you are a wicked man to speak thus of her. No, the truth is that the son of the former Magistrate abandoned her. He is a dog, a son of a pig!"

At another place, some scholars were holding a picnic. Yi Doryung listened and heard them talking.

"These are sad days!" said one of them. "I've heard that a young woman called Choonhyang is to be executed in a few days."

"Oh, this new Magistrate is a wretch!" said another. "But Choonhyang is like the pine and the bamboo which never change. Her only crime was to remain faithful to her betrothed."

All these comments made Yi Doryung hasten into the town.

Meanwhile, Choonhyang, in prison all this time, remained faithful to the memory of Yi Doryung. Gradually, she had grown thin, feeble and sick. But she would not change.

One day, the Magistrate called the attendants and announced to them that in three days he would celebrate a great feast. All the magistrates from nearby towns would be invited.

"On that day," he said, "Choonhyang shall be executed."

When Yi Doryung arrived in the town, he went at once to Choonhyang's home. Her mother did not recognize him.

"Your face reminds me of Yi Doryung, but your dress is that of a beggar," she said. "I do not know who you are."

"I *am* Yi Doryung," he said.

"Ah," sighed the mother. "Every day we have waited for Yi Doryung, but alas, in two or three days Choonhyang will be dead!"

"Listen to me, mother," replied Yi Doryung. "Even though I am a miserable beggar, I love Choonhyang as I always did and I want to see her."

Together they went to the prison. Yi Doryung stood to one side while the mother knocked at the prison window, calling to Choonhyang. After a moment or two, she came and looked out.

"Has anyone seen Yi Doryung?" she asked. "Is there any news of him?"

"A beggar has come to see you," her mother replied. "He claims to be Yi Doryung."

The young man then appeared outside the window. Choonhyang looked at him and recognized her lover.

"Dear Heart!" she cried. "Beggar or not, you are my betrothed. Go back and have a good rest tonight. I must die tomorrow after the feast, but come back in the morning. I wish to have the joy of seeing your dear face again before I am put to death!"

Next morning, when Choonhyang's mother opened the door of the room where Yi Doryung was sleeping, she found that he had already gone. He had risen early and had gone to collect his attendants, all disguised like him, as beggars. Walking together, they went to the palace of the Magistrate. Once there, Yi Doryung managed to get inside the palace. In spite of his beggar's clothes, he even approached the host as the banquet was beginning.

"I am a poor man," he said to the Magistrate, "and I am hungry. Give me something to eat."

The angry official commanded his servants to kick the intruder out. However, one of the servants kindly gave him food and Yi Doryung thanked him with a poem. Upon reading it, the servant felt sure that this was no beggar. He presented the poem to the Magistrate.

"Who wrote this?" the Magistrate demanded. The servant told him it was written by the beggar. He pointed to Yi Doryung.

By this time, the dinner guests began to notice what was going on and to get the idea that this man was really no beggar but, instead, was an important official. He then identified himself as the Envoy of the King, and was immediately treated with great respect.

Yi Doryung first ordered his servants to fetch the prisoner, Choonhyang, so that he might review the case.

They removed the wooden plank from around her neck and brought Choonhyang into the presence of the Envoy who, sitting behind a screen, began his questions. At last he said, "Well, then, if you do not love the Magistrate, will you love *me*? Will you come to me, the King's Envoy? If you refuse, you know, I am entitled to order my men to cut off your head immediately!"

"Alas!" exclaimed Choonhyang. (She did not know who was sitting behind the screen as judge!) "How unhappy are the poor people of this country! You, the Envoy of the King, should help and protect the people. Yet you threaten to condemn to death a poor girl whose only sin is to be faithful!"

Yi Doryung then ordered the servants to untie the cords which bound her hands.

"Now, raise your head," he said. "Look at me."

"No," she exclaimed. "I shall not look at you. I shall not listen to you. My heart belongs to one only!"

Yi Doryung was delighted. He took off his ring and ordered a servant to show it to Choonhyang. When she saw that it was the one she had given to Yi Doryung so long ago, she lifted her eyes and cried out with joy.

"Oh!" she exclaimed. "Yesterday, my beloved was only a beggar, and today he is the King's Envoy!"

Yi Doryung ordered a sedan chair to be brought at once to carry Choonhyang safely home to her mother. The people cheered with joy.

Next, Yi Doryung summoned the wicked Magistrate who had tried to run away.

"The King gave you instructions to feed the people well," he said sternly. "Instead, you feed *upon* them. You have cruelly insulted this faithful woman who is far worthier than you. In the name of the King, I condemn you to forfeit your office!" The people shouted again.

Yi Doryung took his bride to Seoul soon after that. The King was happy to find such faithfulness in a country girl of low birth. He said that the faithfulness of Choonhyang should be a model from that time for all women of Korea, both rich and poor.

(Adapted from *Folk Tales of Old Korea* by Ha, Tae Hung, published by The Korean Information Service, Inc., 31 First St., Taepyong-no, Seoul, Korea, 1958. Reprint permission granted by author, Ha, Tae Hung, Yonsei University Press, Sudaemoon-ku, Seoul, Korea.)

10

THE HEALING WATERS

(From the Iroquois of North America)

What are some of the costs
of loyalty in marriage?

I T WAS WINTER, the snow lay thickly on the ground. There was sorrow among the people, for a dreadful plague was spreading death in the tribe. Everyone had lost a relative, and in some cases whole families had died.

Nekumonta, a handsome young brave, had seen his whole family die before his very eyes—father, mother, brothers and sisters, and even his own children. Powerless to help, he had watched them die one by one. Now the dread disease had laid its awful finger on the brow of his beautiful young wife.

Shanewis, weak and ill, feared that she too must shortly bid her husband farewell and take her departure to the place of the dead. Already she thought she could see her dead children and friends beckoning to her, calling her to join them. When she broke the sad news to Nekumonta his despair was piteous to behold. But after the first outburst of grief he hid his sorrow, being an Iroquois brave.

"I will fight this plague!" he cried. "I will fight it with all my strength!"

Now Nekumonta had heard of some healing herbs, planted by the great Manitou, and sure to heal any disease. The problem was that no one had ever known where Manitou had planted them!

"Wherever they may be, I must find them," said Neku-monta.

So he made his wife comfortable on her couch, covering her with warm furs, and then, embracing her gently, he set out on his long, hard search.

All day he sought eagerly in the forest for the healing herbs, but everywhere the snow lay deep. Not so much as a blade of grass was visible. When night came he crept along the snowy ground, hoping that his sense of smell might aid him in the search. But he could not find the herbs. For three days and nights Nekumonta wandered through the forest, over hills and across rivers, trying to discover the means of curing the malady of beloved Shanewis.

Once he met a little scurrying rabbit and cried eagerly: "Shanewis is dying with the plague. Tell me, where shall I find the herbs which Manitou has planted?"

But the rabbit, friend though he was, hurried away without answering. He knew that the herbs had not yet risen above the ground, and he could not bear to say this to the young brave.

By and by Nekumonta came to the den of his friend, a big bear, and asked the same question. Alas, the bear could give him no reply, and he was obliged to resume his weary journey. All along the way he consulted the beasts of the forest in turn, but he could get no help from any of them. How could they bear to tell him, indeed, that his search was hopeless?

On the third night the young brave was very weak and ill, for he had tasted no food since the beginning of his journey. He was numbed with cold and despair. He stumbled over a dry branch hidden under the snow. He was so tired that he lay where he fell, and immediately went to sleep.

All the birds and the beasts and other creatures that inhabit the forest came to watch over Nekumonta's slumbers. They remembered his kindness to them in former days, how he had never killed an animal unless he really needed it for food or clothing, how he had loved and protected the trees and the flowers. Their hearts were touched by his brave fight for the life of his beautiful Shanewis. They grieved for his misfortunes. They did everything they could do to help in the search, crying to the Great Manitou, and begging him to save Shanewis from the plague which bound her. At last the Great Spirit heard all the crying and responded to their prayers!

While Nekumonta lay asleep, he dreamed that the messenger of Manitou came to him. In the dream he saw his beautiful Shanewis, pale and thin, but lovely as ever. As he looked she smiled at him, and sang a strange, sweet song, like the murmuring of a distant waterfall.

Suddenly the scene seemed to change, and it really was a waterfall he heard. In musical language it called him by name, saying: "Seek us, O Nekumonta, and when you find us Shanewis shall live. We are the Healing Waters of the Great Manitou!"

Nekumonta awoke with the words of the song still ringing in his ears. Rising to his feet he looked in every direction. But there was no water to be seen, and only the faint murmuring sound of a waterfall was to be heard. He fancied he could even distinguish words in it.

"Release us!" they seemed to say. "Set us free, and then Shanewis shall be saved!" But Nekumonta searched in vain for the waters. How could he release them, when he could not find them?

Suddenly it occurred to him that the sound was coming from down underneath his feet. The waters must be underground! Seizing branches, stones, and flints, he dug feverishly into the earth. He dug and dug until he was exhausted. But at last the hidden spring was disclosed. Then he saw, almost hidden under the snow, what he had missed before, the waters trickling down the vale, carrying life and happiness wherever they went.

The young brave bathed his aching limbs in the healing stream, and in a moment he was well and strong! Raising his hands he gave thanks to Manitou.

Raising his hands he gave thanks. ...

After this, with trembling, eager fingers, he made a jar of clay from the bank of the stream. He then made a fire to bake it in, so that he might carry life to Shanewis. As he finally pursued his way homeward with his treasure, Nekumonta's despair was changed to rejoicing. He sped like the wind!

When he reached the village, his friends came running to greet him, their faces sad and hopeless. The plague still raged there. Quickly Nekumonta told them about the Healing Waters, and begged them to run and be healed. They ran, with new hope.

He found Shanewis on the verge of the Shadow-land, and scarcely able to murmur a farewell to her husband.

But Nekumonta did not take time to listen to her broken words. Quickly he poured some of the Healing Water between the parched lips, bathed her hands, and her brow, until she fell into a gentle slumber. When she awoke the fever had gone away. She was serene and smiling, and the hearts of both were filled with a great happiness.

The tribe was forever rid of the dreaded plague, and the people gave to Nekumonta the title of "Chief of the Healing Waters" so that all might know that it was he who had brought them the gift of Manitou.

(Retold from Lewis Spence, *Myths and Legends: The North American Indians,* published by David D. Nickerson and Company, Boston, in 1914.)

Stories About Reward
and Punishment

11

WATER OVER THE WORLD

(From Greece)

To what extent are natural disasters
punishment for wrong-doing?

I N THE FAR-OFF TIMES OF LONG AGO, it is said that the gods
came and went freely on the earth, taking pleasure in the
mountains and valleys, woodlands and meadows. Sometimes
people recognized them as gods, but more often they thought
that the gods were other people like themselves.

But as the years went by, people of the earth grew careless
and selfish. After they discovered how to melt metal and
make beautiful jewelry and vases, they began to gather up
riches for themselves. Families became greedy about their
own possessions, and each family wished to be the richest in
all the world. Brothers and sisters, even, could not trust each
other. They were all busy taking care of themselves and their
own possessions. Of course, they couldn't welcome strangers
any longer, and they closed their doors and locked them
against beggars. Everybody was afraid.

Some of the gods and goddesses, looking down from
Mount Olympus, saw the cruel and greedy ways of the people
and complained about them to Zeus, the king. "Those wicked
people ought to be taught a lesson!" they said to Zeus.

Zeus thought for a long time and finally agreed to go
down himself and look over the earth.

"I'll go in the form of a beggar," he said, "and I'll go from door to door asking for a bed to sleep in and for food. Maybe I can find at least one person who will be kind to strangers." And he added, "I'll take Hermes along with me." (Hermes was Zeus' favorite messenger.)

So the two gods went down to earth and for many days they wandered over hills and valleys through many lands. But wherever they went, they were turned away. There was no one who would welcome them and no one offered them food or shelter for the night.

At last, Zeus shook his head sadly and said to Hermes, "We've seen enough. All the people on earth seem to be deceitful and cruel and willing to do anything to get money. There doesn't seem to be a decent man among them. Not a single one of them will welcome a stranger. Let's go back to Olympus. Tomorrow I will send a rain to wash the earth away. It will be such a rain as has not been seen since the world was made. The whole human race will be destroyed by flood. I am sick and tired of their selfish ways!"

"If this is your will, Father Zeus," Hermes said, "then so be it. But let us wait one more day. There's just a chance we may find one good person whom we may save from drowning when the floods come."

Zeus nodded. "You have spoken well, Hermes!" he said. "We shall wait one more day."

So Zeus and Hermes wandered one more day over the plains and hills, seeking a person who would welcome them. At night-fall, they came to a small hut, thatched with reeds and straw. An old man named Deucalion lived there with his wife, Pyrrha.

Deucalion and Pyrrha had no money at all. They lived on what Deucalion could produce by working in his field and small vineyard. But they were satisfied with what they had and welcomed the strangers into their home. The two gods had to stoop to enter the low door, but Deucalion did not seem to notice.

"We haven't much," he said, "but we can give you clean lodging and simple food. It's the best we have. And we can tell you stories. We have always liked stories ourselves."

The two gods were delighted with the stories and with the simple, good food. That night they slept well on the hard beds in Deucalion and Pyrrha's little house. When they were about to leave the next morning, Zeus thanked them, without telling them that he and Hermes were both gods.

"You have been fine hosts," he said.

"Well," said Deucalion, "it is little we have to offer to guests but we can always make them welcome."

"Good friends," answered Zeus, "the king of gods and men will surely reward you for your hospitality."

Deucalion looked puzzled, but at that moment a glory shown around the faces of the two strangers. Deucalion and Pyrrha now knew that their guests were more than mere men. Then Zeus told of the plan which he had made to send a flood of waters over the whole earth.

"All other people will be destroyed for their selfishness," he said, "but you two are to be saved. You are to build a boat of strong oak beams and store it full of food and household goods. Then shut yourselves in the boat. This is the only way you can escape the anger of the gods."

When Zeus had finished speaking, a peal of thunder shook the sky and the two gods vanished into the air.

For six days Deucalion and Pyrrha worked busily at the building of the boat. Their neighbors grew curious and asked what they were doing. When they heard about the great flood which would be coming, the neighbors laughed.

"But Zeus himself has said so!" Deucalion insisted.

They only laughed again and went their way, back to the business of collecting wealth for themselves.

On the seventh day when the boat was finished, Deucalion went in with his wife, Pyrrha, and shut the door fast. Zeus, watching from Olympus, saw the door of the boat close and immediately he opened the windows of the sky and let the floods fall on the earth. It rained without stopping for nine days and nine nights. The oceans and lakes and rivers rose and covered the plains, then the hillsides, and then even the tops of the mountains.

Of course, all the human beings living on the earth had to be drowned. But Zeus made it possible for some of every kind of wild animal and bird, great and small, to find refuge on the highest trees of the highest hilltops.

All this time the boat, with Deucalion and Pyrrha safe inside, drifted over the top of the waters until finally it came to rest on the very peak of the high Mount Parnassus. And then, after nine days, Zeus at last shut up the windows of the sky and the rain stopped. After that he made a mighty wind blow out of the east, which drove the waters before it out into the farthest parts of the ocean. It blew for a hundred days and a hundred nights, until both hills and valleys were dry land once more.

As soon as the water had gone down, Deucalion opened a window in the side of the boat. When he and Pyrrha looked out, they saw the waters lowering and the dry land on the tops of the mountains around them. They came out of the boat and gave thanks to Zeus for their safety.

As soon as they could, they went out onto the mountain side and walked around. It was lonely on the earth without any other people and their hearts were sad. Daily, as the waters lowered, they wandered farther down the mountain side until one evening they came to a deep rocky glen and found a cave in the side of the mountain. That night they lay down in the cave to sleep and as they slept they both dreamed the same dream.

Both dreamed that a woman stood before them. Her face was veiled and she spoke softly to them these strange words, "If you want to see human faces about you once more, O Deucalion and Pyrrha, you must take and throw behind you

It was lonely on the earth without any other people, and their hearts were sad:

the bones of your Great Mother."

Then they both woke up to find it was day. They told each other of their dream, surprised that they had dreamed the same thing, and a little troubled.

"What could it mean—the bones of our Great Mother?" they asked each other. "Where can we find those bones? Who is the Great Mother?"

At last Deucalion thought he understood.

"Surely," he said, "the Earth is our Great Mother, for we were made out of her. And the bones—they must be the rocks and stones!"

Then Deucalion and Pyrrha went out quickly from the cave and began to gather armfuls of stones, which they flung, one by one, backwards over their shoulders.

All at once, the stones that they threw became people. The ones Decualion threw became men, and those Pyrrha threw became women. And this was the way that a new race of human beings came into life, to people the earth once more.

After all this had happened, Deucalion went back to the land where he and Pyrrha had lived as poor farmers. They took with them some of the new people that Zeus had made of the stones of the earth. They built a great city in the familiar land and ruled there as peaceful and just rulers in a kingdom where strangers were welcomed, beggars were fed, and people trusted each other.

(This retelling of the Greek flood story by Sophia Lyon Fahs was found among her papers with no indication of the date of writing or the sources used. Its main features agree with the account of "Deucalion's Flood," as given on pp. 138-39 of *The Greek Myths,* by Robert Graves, Vol. I New York: George Brazilier, 1957, but an earlier source was obviously used.)

12
MAN IS PUNISHED
BY THE ANIMALS
(From the Cherokees of North America)

To what extent is getting sick
a punishment for wrong-doing?

W HEN THIS STORY WAS FIRST TOLD the Cherokee Indians,
lived in the mountains of North and South Carolina.
They did not know what we do today about the germs
which make us sick. They imagined that unseen spirits flew
around carrying diseases. They believed too that some animals were more than animals and that they had powers
beyond the powers of men. It was natural that the Cherokees
once supposed that animals-greater-than-animals held the
unseen spirits under their control and could send them like
arrows into persons or other animals.

When someone became sick, the medicine man, who was a
man more powerful than other men, was called to come to
the wigwam. Then, by magic, he would decide which of the
animals had become angry and had sent the sickness. The
medicine man would then make prayers and give gifts to this
animal and beg it to send the sickness away. If he were not
successful, he would try again to use his magic. But now the
story:

In the far-off days of long, long ago, the Cherokee Indians
imagined that people and animals could understand each
other's ways of talking. They imagined, too, that the birds

64

could talk with one another as well as with people and that insects and worms also talked together. In that far off time, it was thought that all the animals and birds and all living creatures lived happily together on the earth.

They imagined, too, that the birds could talk with one another. ...

But, as the number of people and animals and birds increased, it became harder and harder for so many living creatures to find enough food to satisfy them. They began chasing each other out of the best places for food. Many animals were required to move about so often that they were kept busy simply hunting new places to build their homes. Some animals went hungry.

People and animals were no longer the good friends they had been. People learned how to make tools such as bows and arrows. They learned how to sharpen stones and knives and clubs. With these weapons they could go out into the forests when they were hungry and kill a few animals and eat them. The animals were angry and frightened. Things must not go on in this way or else they all might perish. What could they do? Finally they met to consult together for their common safety.

First, the bears met to discuss what they could do. Old Chief White Bear had charge of the council. "What shall we do to keep the humans from killing us and our brothers and sisters?" asked Chief White Bear.

"We must fight humans with their own weapons," said one of the bears. "We must make bows and arrows and go out and shoot them, just as they have been shooting at us."

"Is there any bear who knows how these bows and arrows are made?" asked Chief White Bear.

One of the bears stood up and shook his head. Then he said, "Humans use a part of the skin of a dead bear to make the string for his bow. If we are to make bows, one of us must be killed." He dropped his head and was quiet for a few moments. Finally he stood up on his two hind feet and said, "I will give my life so that a bow may have a string."

So it was—a bear was killed.

At last the bow was finished and Young Bear ran with it out into the forest. Soon he saw a man creeping up through the trees, ready to shoot. Young Bear tried to pull back the string of his bow, but he couldn't pull it back! His claws caught in the string so that he could not make the arrow fly.

Sadly Young Bear went back to report to Chief White Bear. "I can't pull the string back. My claws get in the way," he said.

"What shall we do?" Chief White Bear asked.

Young Bear thought a moment. Then he spoke again. "I

will give up my claws," he said. "Then one of us at least will be able to use the bow and arrow."

Chief White Bear shook his head. "Human weapons are not for us," he said. "Already one of us has given his life to string the bow. But I shall not allow another to give his claws. Our claws are our weapons. We must keep them. We must think of a better plan."

But none of the bears could think of anything better. At last the council was dismissed.

The next animals to meet to try to work on the problem were the deer. They met with their chief who was named Chief Little Deer. Many suggestions were made, but none seemed likely to work. It began to look as though the council of the deer would be as unsuccessful as the council of the bears.

At last Chief Little Deer rose and spoke. All the deer crowded closer to hear every word. "People need to kill some of us in order to eat," said Chief Little Deer slowly and thoughtfully. "We can't stop them. If they do not eat, they will die. But we can make them show us some respect. We can tell them that before a person kills one of us that person ought to ask our forgiveness. The killer should say to the deer, 'I am sorry to do this.' "And from now on," said Chief Little Deer, "I will wander through the forest and when I see that someone has just shot one of us, I will go to where the deer lies. As the spirit is about to leave its body, I will bend over it and ask, 'Did the person who killed you beg your pardon?' If the deer says 'Yes,' the person will be forgiven. But if that person did not ask forgiveness, we will bring sickness. The person will have so much pain and lameness that there can be no more hunting. We shall call the illness 'rheumatism.'"

The deer all nodded their approval. One of them was sent at once to tell people what had been planned. And thus the council of the deer broke up.

Not long after this, the fish and the snakes met together and they discussed humans, the hunters. They asked themselves why people did not like fish and snakes and talked of how they had been treating them. Finally this council made a plan.

"We shall punish people," they said. "When they have been doing cruel things to us, we will make them have bad dreams. In their dreams, huge snakes will coil around them. Or perhaps they will dream that they are eating fish that have spoiled in the sun!" This is what they planned for humans.

But animals and fish were not the only ones who were angry at people. A few days later, another council met, presided over by the grubworm. This council was made up of the birds, the insects, and the smaller animals. There were many of them at the meeting, each with a special complaint.

"People are very cruel to me," said the frog. "They kick me and step on me and push me about. I do not like it."

"They are even more cruel to us birds," said one of them. "They catch us in traps; they tie our feet together; they roast us over the fire. We do not like it."

"You are all complaining over little things," said the ground squirrel suddenly. "People are not all evil as you seem to think. They do many kind things. . . ." But before the squirrel could finish, the other animals jumped on it and clawed it. They would not listen to anything good about their enemy.

Finally one animal had an idea, and said, "We must invent sickness. When people do these things to us, we must make them sick. We will think of many diseases. These will be the punishment."

So the animals thought up many kinds of sicknesses. They invented headaches; they invented fevers; they invented malaria—in fact, all the diseases known in the world today were planned in that animal council. Grubworm, who was chairman of the council, became more and more delighted as each disease was invented.

After a long time the animals, the birds, and the insects were satisfied with the punishments they had planned. Not till then did council meetings stop. And this is the way sickness and disease began.

But this is not the end of the story. There is another part of it, about how the plants came to man's rescue. The plants were more friendly to man than were the animals. They heard what the animals had planned. The story was passed along from one plant to another and each plant tried to think of something that could be done to help man.

Finally the plants got together to talk over their ideas. They had a council—something like the councils which the animals had been having. After they had talked it over, one of the plants proposed a plan that would at least lessen the evil which the animals had planned. Each tree, each shrub, each herb, even the simplest grass and moss, agreed to furnish a remedy for one of the sicknesses which the animals had invented.

One shrub said, "If someone comes down with malaria and boils my leaves and drinks the water they were boiled in, the person will be cured."

Then another said the same about its flowers and another about its roots. Every plant had something to offer. There would always be a plant to say, "I will help people if they call on me when they are sick."

So it was that sickness came into the world. So it was also that medicines were made—long ago. The plants are still very useful to us. We boil their leaves and crush their stems and eat their fruits. And even today when people call doctors to help in times of sickness, many kinds of plants are gathered. Their leaves and flowers are mashed and boiled to press out their juices. The juices are used as medicine. One of these is the castor oil plant, which almost everyone has at some time taken as medicine.

(Retold from "Myths of the Cherokee," by James Mooney, *Nineteenth Annual Report of the U.S. Bureau of American Ethnology,* 1897-1898, Part 1, pp. 250-252.)

13

NIYAK AND THE EAGLE
(From the Eskimos of North America)

Why is it important to keep promises?

ONCE UPON A TIME, there was an Eskimo boy named Niyak, who lived in a village far north on the Bering Sea coast. Niyak's father had been taken by the Old Man of the Sea as he hunted for seals. His mother too had died when Niyak was small. But the boy was not lonely as he grew up because he lived with his wise old grandmother. She knew about as much as most of the medicine men.

Niyak had a special friend, a beautiful girl named Umuk, whose father was the very best hunter in all of Eskimo land. Umuk liked the orphan boy and often invited him to gather berries with her, or to hunt for birds' eggs in the spring.

One day Umuk invited Niyak to gather grass. "You know we need the grass for making mats to keep the boats dry," she reminded him.

Niyak agreed to go for a while, but he said his grandmother would be expecting him back home rather soon. "We'll have to gather fast," he told her.

Umuk said that was all right and offered to gather her grass on one side of the hill while he gathered on the other.

The time seemed to pass very fast, but Niyak was careful and knew exactly when it was time for them to go back. "Umuk," he called. "It's time to go home!"

"In a minute," she called back from the other side of the

hill. "I need just a little more grass to make my bundle large enough."

Niyak lay on his back on the hillside, looking into the sky and watching the birds, while he waited for Umuk. He could hear her busily pulling grass. Suddenly, he could no longer hear her. He walked around the little hill, but Umuk was not there. It seemed the earth must have swallowed her up!

All afternoon Niyak called and called. As night came, he returned to the village and went right away to her father. They both went back then to search for Umuk together. They searched all night. No Umuk! Not even a trace!

That day Umuk's father gathered all the medicine men in the village to see if they could help to find his little girl. They were frightened and concerned. They even sang songs and danced strange dances to try to find the answer to the problem. But nothing happened! At last, Niyak thought of his grandmother, who was wiser than many of the medicine men. So he went to her and asked her to help.

"Yes," she said. "I think I can help you, if you will do just as I tell you."

The old woman directed the hunter to make a pair of snowshoes for Niyak and an Eskimo walking stick so that he might feel his way over the ice and snow. Then she said his wife must make a rainproof parka of seal skin and some gloves of fish scales. This was so Niyak would not get wet in the land of the fog. But most important of all, she said, was a knapsack for him. It should be made of the skin of the swan with all the feathers in it. When all these things were made for Niyak, he went back to the old grandmother.

Together, with all the people of the village, they went to the Kashim, the center for village ceremonies, where there were two big drums of walrus gut.

"Now, beat as hard as you can," said the grandmother to the medicine man, and they all beat the drums with all their might.

"Now, bring food," she said. They brought in two large clam shells full and placed them in the knapsack at her direction. "Now, put on all your new things," she said to Niyak.

"Even the snowshoes?" he asked in wonder. (It was not snowing at all, for it was midsummer and the grass was green.)

"Put on your snowshoes, too," she said firmly.

Finally, Niyak was ready to go, fully dressed in the new rain parka of sealskin and the fishskin gloves. He placed the knapsack on his back and stepped towards the porch of the Kashim. But just then, his feet began to rise from the floor so that he walked out on the air while the drums played furiously. He could hear the shouts of the people down below, although he could no longer see them through the clouds.

Niyak flew first to the hill where Umuk had been lost. To his surprise, he could see tracks there leading up to the sky. He could follow them easily until he came to the clouds. As he pushed into the first big cloud, he could see a door in the sky, almost like the door of an igloo. He pushed it open and looked inside. There was only fog. He could not see two steps in front of himself and he could no longer see the tracks that he had been following.

"I wonder what I should do now," he said to himself.

Suddenly, Niyak felt something move at his back. It was his swanskin packsack with the feathers. "K-l-o-o-k, k-l-o-o-k," it said. "I will help you, little Niyak."

Coming down from his back, the swan stood beside him on the ground in the land of fog. "Ah, here are the tracks," she said, pointing to the ground around his feet. Niyak's eyes were getting used to the fog now and, sure enough, he could see the tracks the swan pointed out.

"You must follow them," she said. "I will stay with you and direct you so that you won't get lost in the fog. When you hear me call, you will know that you have lost the tracks and my voice will guide you back."

So Niyak started through the wet fog, feeling his way with the stick Umuk's father had made. He was very glad to have the fishskin gloves and the rain parka, for it was cold and wet in the fog. He could not see a thing, not even the tracks he was trying to follow.

Suddenly, he heard the swan say "K-l-o-o-k" and he knew he had lost the tracks. He turned toward the sound of the swan. He went on for some distance and then heard the swan again. This time it called him to the left, so he went on.

All at once, because he could not see ahead of him, he bumped into another little door. He pushed it open. "Surely, this is the most beautiful land I have ever seen!" he exclaimed to himself. There were blue lakes and many berries. The sun shone warmly and there were many trees with fruits of all colors on them.

In the distance, he saw a strange-looking tree, with a flat top, such as he had never seen before. Going up closer to look at it, he saw that the strange flat tree was really a giant bird's nest. Filled with curiosity, he climbed up to look inside the nest.

"Why, what is this?" he asked. There were five little birds in the nest! Niyak knew they must be eagles, although he had never seen an eagle. One of the birds was very tiny, with feathers of all the colors in the world growing on its wings. Niyak thought it was the most beautiful little bird he had ever seen.

He noticed that the eagle's nest was not very clean so, because he was a neat boy and had been taught by his wise grandmother, he decided to do some housecleaning before leaving the nest. He pushed the five young eagles over into one corner, careful not to frighten them, and began to clean out the trash.

Then came a big surprise. Down in the very bottom of the nest, he found a lot of old wet leaves. When he pushed up the last of the leaves, he felt something round and hard under his hand. "It feels like somebody's head!" Niyak exclaimed.

Carefully, he began trying to lift the round thing out. He found it was indeed a head. It belonged to little Umuk, buried down in the wet leaves.

"Are you all right, little Umuk?" he cried. "Are you alive?"

Umuk could not speak right then, but she opened her eyes and tried to smile.

'You must be weak and hungry!" he exclaimed. Taking hold of her arms, Niyak drew her out of the nest as quickly as he could without hurting her. Then he took out of his knapsack the two clam shells full of food for the little girl. Soon she felt better and began to try to speak.

"You came just in time," she said. "I thought I would be left to die there!"

Suddenly, while they were talking, they heard a queer loud noise, a sort of whir, overhead. A giant eagle whizzed down from the sky, alighting on the edge of the nest. Niyak and Umuk huddled back in terror.

"Don't worry," said the eagle. "I won't hurt you." Raising up his great horned beak, he took the skin off as if it were a mask. The eagle had the face of a man. "I won't hurt you," he repeated. "I just want to thank whoever came here and cleaned up my nest. It's been needing some cleaning for a long time."

Niyak poked his head out from behind a tree, not quite sure whether or not he dared trust the great bird with a human face.

"Please come out where I can see you," said the Man-Eagle. "I'm really very grateful to you!"

Then Niyak and Umuk both stepped out in front of the tree, but still neither one dared to speak.

"You may take the little girl with you," the eagle said to Niyak, "and because you have cleaned my nest so nicely, I will give you one of my own eagle children."

Niyak was glad to get a little eagle, for he had always

wanted one. "I would like to have the smallest baby," he said. "I'd like the little one with all the pretty feathers."

The Eagle looked disappointed. "I'd really rather not let you have the baby," he said. "I'm very fond of the little one. But of course I've made a promise, so you shall have it. But not right away. The baby must learn to fly first."

"How long will that be?" asked Niyak.

"Five years," said the Eagle. "You must go back to the earth and five years from today I will bring the baby eagle to you."

"It seems rather a long time," Niyak said. "I hope you won't forget."

"I won't forget," the Eagle promised. "But I must warn you never to let any person on earth know about this, or see the baby eagle when I bring it. If any earth person learns about this, the baby will come back to me and you will never see it again."

So Niyak took the little girl, put her inside his parka where she would not get cold and wet in the fog, and set off for the earth again. It was not far to the door opening into the fog land.

Suddenly, he heard a familiar sound. "K-l-o-o-k, k-l-o-o-k." It was the swan calling to show the way. Quickly Niyak and Umuk set off in the direction of the voice. It became louder until at last they came to the big white swan perched on a hummock of grass right by the door which would lead into the next beautiful land.

"Thank you so much," Niyak told the swan. "I have little Umuk here in my parka. We are going back to the world below. Do you want to go with us?"

"No," replied the swan. "I shall stay here and direct other people through the fog."

"Well, goodbye, then," Niyak said, as he pushed open the door out of the fog land and looked into the land beyond it. He could see the tracks plainly now where he had been before. So on he went, with little Umuk tucked under his cape, down to where they could see the hill where they had picked grass the day before. They hurried now to the village, where they could hear the drums beating. Niyak's snowshoes did not touch the earth, as he walked through the air.

Suddenly, the whole crowd down below was stunned into silence. At last someone spoke, "It is Niyak."

"Niyak is back again!" the crowd cried out. "But where is little Umuk? He has failed to find little Umuk!"

"But what is that sticking out from under his parka?" asked someone.

"It looks like two little shoes!" several cried.

Niyak said not a word. He circled in the air around the Kashim until he came to the place where Umuk's father and mother were standing. Then, reaching beneath his parka, he took out little Umuk and handed her over to her mother.

Umuk's mother laughed and cried. Her father laughed and cried. The whole crowd burst into a roar. Little Umuk was back!

It was a great celebration. A great feast was held in the Kashim for the two young people. Games were played. The medicine men sang their best songs and did their best tricks. Niyak's grandmother was honored above them all because it was her advice which had helped Niyak to find little Umuk. Then at last, when the celebration was over, the people went back to their work.

Niyak grew tall and handsome and became a hunter like Umuk's father. Umuk grew, too, and became very lovely. The old grandmother died and they beat the drums for twelve days. Many things happened. But Niyak never forgot the eagle's promise.

At the end of five years, he went away from the village, where no one could see him, and watched for two days. He saw nothing, and returned to his home again. The next day he went out and the next. The eagle did not appear. Niyak wondered if he had forgotten his promise. "I'll give him one more chance," Niyak said to himself. "I'll go back tomorrow."

The next day was bright and fine. Niyak walked far from the village and sat down on the tundra. He had not been there long when he saw two large clouds in the sky. They seemed to be moving closer to him. As the clouds drew nearer, he saw that they were not clouds at all, but two great eagles. One of the eagles carried a giant seal called a mukluk in one of his talons. In the other, he held a deer. Both of these he dropped in front of Niyak and then both eagles alighted on the ground beside him.

Lifting back his face like a mask, the same eagle Niyak had seen five years before spoke to him. "I am bringing you my son as I promised. He is just like me. Every day he will hunt for you. He will bring you more game than you can eat. You must remember always to come far out from the village to meet him. If anyone else sees him, you will never see him again."

Then both eagles flew away and Niyak took the fine deer and the mukluk or seal, home with him.

After that, any time he wanted meat, Niyak walked far out from the village and the young eagle brought food to him. Sometimes it would be a deer or a seal. The eagle was so big and powerful that he even brought Niyak a walrus or a whale once in a while. Everyone in the village said Niyak must be a great hunter.

One day, as Niyak walked out to meet the eagle, he said to himself, "Why should I walk so far?" So he sat down on the ground much closer to the village than ever before. Soon he saw the eagle coming. It swooped down low and dropped a fat caribou at Niyak's feet. As it flew away, a man at the village looked out and saw the eagle. He called to all the people. They ran out of their igloos to look at the giant bird.

Niyak picked up his meat and carried it home. "This is

much better," he said to himself, "than walking so far and carrying the heavy meat."

The next time Niyak needed meat he walked out from the village and sat down. Soon he saw not only his eagle approaching, but another which looked just like him. They alighted near him on the ground. One of them lifted up his face like a mask. He spoke, "You broke your promise to me and you did not go far from the village. The people there saw my son, so he will never come back to you again." Together, the two eagles flew away.

"You broke your promise to me."

Niyak went away from the village several times when he was hungry. He sat down and waited, but the eagle did not return. After that, he had to hunt on foot as did the other Eskimos and worked much harder than he had ever worked before.

Although this happened many, many years ago before the white man ever came to Alaska, even today when an Eskimo breaks his promise the others will say to him, "Remember how Niyak broke his promise because he was too lazy to walk far? He had to work hard all the rest of his life!" Even in Eskimo land, it is very bad to break a promise.

(Adapted from *Medicine Men of Hooper Bay: More Tales from the Clapping Mountains of Alaska,* by Charles Gillham; New York: Macmillan Co., 1955.) Reprint permission granted by Macmillan Publishing Co., Inc. Copyright C.E. Gillham, 1955.

14

THE BOY WHO WENT TO THE SKY

(From the Cherokees of North America)

Why is it wrong to cheat?

I N THE ANCIENT TIMES, before there was even a moon to light the sky, there was a boy who was known everywhere as the best ballplayer in his village. He could catch well, run swiftly to the goal, and almost never did he lose a game for his side. We do not know his name, but we will call him Watadin, meaning "skilled with the ball."

One season the village of Watadin decided to play a ball game with another village of the Cherokees from the other side of the ridge. The two teams met not far from a mountain called Pilot Knob and the game began.

Of course, the boy Watadin, proud of his skill, was anxious to help win the game for his side and played with all his might. But for a while everything seemed to be going against him. Time and time again, the players from the other village ran and made the goal.

"My village must make the goal!" Watadin thought.

So then he did a thing which is absolutely forbidden in the rules of ball playing. Instead of kicking the ball, as the Indians do, Watadin picked it up and threw it with his hands. No one seemed to notice, and he thought no one had seen because the ball went straight to the goal as he wanted it to.

But then the boys and girls who sat in a wide circle on the

grassy field to watch the game saw a strange thing. Bounding away from the goal, the ball went straight up into the air and following the ball went the boy who had cheated! His feet left the ball field. He seemed to be leaping up toward the sky to try to bring back the ball, but neither the boy nor the ball could stop. Up, up, higher and farther through the blue air they went until the ball was out of sight and the boy could no longer be seen.

Up to that time not a word had been said, but when this happened the people rubbed their eyes in wonder. Some of them looked at each other. They went silently home then and decided among themselves that this was a lesson, for some of the boys had noticed the cheating. They decided that the Great Spirit must have seen and taken the boy out of the game.

But that night another strange thing happened. Sitting late beside their campfire, the braves of all the villages of the Cherokee country saw a huge round ball of silver rise in the sky and then hang there, lighting up the sky and the tops of the trees with its wonderful pale light. On the surface of this ball of silver could be seen the face of the boy who had cheated in the ball game.

The moon had come to the heavens! It was the ball, which could always be seen from that time, sometimes very slim, sometimes round and full. When it was round they could see Watadin, the boy.

The people agreed that Watadin had learned a lesson. "The Great Spirit has taught Watadin to be truthful," they said. "Now he can tell us things we did not understand about the sky, the sun, the storms with their thunder, and the rainbow."

Sometimes they saw that the moon was smaller and that sometimes it was eclipsed. When that happened, the night would suddenly darken and the tribes would gather and beat the drums. They thought that the eclipse came because a

...the braves of all the villages of the Cherokee country saw a huge round ball of silver rise in the sky...

great frog had tried to swallow the moon, but that the drums had frightened it away.

The oddest thing about the moon was its way of waxing and waning. From night to night it would be so large that they could easily see the boy in the moon. Then it would be nothing but a silver thread in the sky above the pine trees.

This happened, the boy told them, to remind all ball-players never to cheat. When the moon looked small and pale, it was because someone had handled a ball unfairly. So it came about in the Cherokee country that they played ball after that only in the full of the moon.

(This story comes from *Stories From an Indian Cave,* by Carolyn Sherwin Bailey. Chicago: Albert Whitman & Company, 1924. Reprinted with permission of the publishers.)

Stories About Conflict Over Power and Possessions

15

A DRUM
TO DANCE BY
(From the Bakongo in Africa)

How should we decide who owns what?

N ZAMBI, THE GODDESS WHO CREATED THE WORLD, is a familiar character in many of the ancient West African myths. Some readers today may be confused because Nzambi and her followers seem to be people, rather than gods and animals. The fact is that ancient storytellers often concealed their human characters by calling them something else. In this story, the animal followers of Nzambi certainly represent people, and deal with their creator as though she also were human. It is a little difficult for people to understand it today, but for the early Africans there was no problem. And here is the story:

When the goddess Nzambi Mpungu made the world, she provided everything she could think of for the people in it. But she forgot that they would need a drum to dance by.

In those days, people and animals and birds all had tails. They were much alike or even the same. It happened that in a village near the home of the goddess Nzambi, there lived a little bird with a long tail named Nchonzo. His tail was always beating on the earth and this beating gave Nchonzo an idea. That was how he happened to set to work to make a drum.

When Nchonzo finished his drum, he called some of his

And since Neambi had made the world in the first place, she thought the drum belonged to her.

friends together and beat the drum so they could dance. He beat it so loudly that Nzambi the goddess heard and wanted to dance too. And since Nzambi had made the world in the first place, she thought the drum belonged to her.

"What about this?" she demanded of her people. "I, a great princess, cannot dance because I have no drum, but that little wagtail bird dances! Go now, O Antelope, and tell Nchonzo that Nzambi the goddess wants the drum."

So the antelope went to Wagtail and asked him to send the drum to Nzambi. But Nchonzo refused.

"No, indeed," he said. "I can't give the drum to Nzambi because I made it myself and it's mine!"

"But Nzambi gave you life," the antelope reminded him. "She made you. Surely, you owe her something in return."

"Yes, that's true," Nchonzo admitted. "But I can't give her my drum!"

"Well, then, lend it to me," said the antelope. "I'd like to play on it a little myself."

"Certainly," Nchonzo agreed. "But not to keep."

So Antelope took the drum and went off by himself to beat it. After beating for a short time, he noticed that Nchonzo was not looking so he ran away with the drum.

As soon as Wagtail noticed that Antelope had gone off with his drum, he was very angry. He sent his friends after the thief. They soon caught the antelope, killed him and brought the drum back to Nchonzo.

The goddess Nzambi, of course, wondered why Antelope was so long returning from his mission. Finally she sent Hyena to see what was the matter. When Hyena brought back word of Antelope's death, she grieved and was sorry, but she still wanted the drum.

"Well, then," she said to the wild ox, "will you, Ox, please go and get the drum from Wagtail, so that I can dance?"

But Ox tried the same game as Antelope and met with the same fate. Again Hyena went to see what was the matter and returned with bad news. She told how Ox had tried to run away with the drum, but had been caught and killed. Nzambi grieved, but she still wanted the drum. She cried out to all her followers. She asked someone to please get her Wagtail's drum.

At last, Small Ant stood out from among the people and volunteered. "Don't weep, O Nzambi," said Ant. "I will get that drum for you."

Nzambi was doubtful. "You are such a small creature," she said. "How can *you* get the drum?"

Small Ant laughed. "I can do it because I *am* so small," she said. "I won't be noticed!"

So the ant went to Wagtail's town and waited outside Nchonzo's house until everybody inside was sound asleep. Then she entered the house, quickly found the drum, carried it away, and finally brought it to the goddess Nzambi.

Nzambi was delighted. She rewarded the ant at once. She then began to beat the drum for all her followers to dance by.

Over in his own village, Nchonzo heard the noise of the beating and shouting. He said to his followers, "Listen! They are dancing in Nzambi's village. But they haven't any drum to dance by! How did they get a drum?"

Then he thought quickly. "They must have stolen mine!" he exclaimed. "Let's look for it." When they looked all through his house for the drum, they found that, sure enough, it was gone.

Nchonzo, the wagtail, was very angry, and called the birds together at once. They all came to hear what he had to say, except the pigeon.

After the birds had discussed the matter, they decided to send a messenger to Nzambi, asking her to appoint a place of meeting where they might talk about the problem. Nzambi suggested that they all go to the town of Prince Neamlau and talk it over before him. Nchonzo, the wagtail, agreed. He and his followers went to Neamlau's town to wait for the goddess. Two days they waited. On the third day Nzambi and her people arrived.

As first speaker, Nchonzo said, "O Prince! I made a drum and Nzambi has taken it from me. It is for her to tell you why. Let her speak."

Then the goddess Nzambi arose and said, "O Prince! My people wished to dance, but we had no drum and therefore they could not. Now I heard the sound of a drum being beaten in the village over which I had set Nchonzo to rule. I therefore sent first the antelope as my ambassador to Nchonzo to ask him for the drum and my ambassador was killed. I then sent the wild ox for the drum, but he also was killed. Finally, I sent Small Ant and she brought me the drum. My people danced and were happy. Surely, O Prince, I who brought forth all the living in the world have a right to this drum if I want it!"

Prince Neamlau and his old men, having heard all that was said, retired to drink water. When they returned, Neamlau was ready to speak.

"You have asked me to decide this question," he said, "and my judgment is this: It is true that Nzambi is the mother of us all, but Nchonzo, the wagtail, certainly made the drum. Now, when the goddess Nzambi made us all, she left us free to live as we choose. She did not give us drums at our birth. The drums we made ourselves. They are therefore ours, just as we may be said to be Nzambi's. If she had made drums and sent them into the world with us, then the drums would be hers. But she did not. Therefore, she was wrong to take the drum from Nchonzo, the wagtail."

Nzambi, the goddess, then paid Nchonzo, the wagtail, for the drum and she was fined for her mistake in stealing it. Then both Nzambi and Nchonzo gave presents to Prince Neamlau and went their way.

("A Drum to Dance By" is adapted from *Notes on the Folklore of the Fjort* by R. E. Dennet, Publications of the Folklore Society, XLI, London, 1898.)

16

THE CHIEF OF
THE WELL
(From Haiti)

To whom does the water belong?

T HERE WAS ONCE A DROUGHT in the country. The streams
dried up and the wells went dry. There was no place
for anybody to get water. The animals met to discuss the
situation—the cow, the dog, the goat, the horse, the donkey,
and all the others. They decided to ask God for help.
Together they went to God and told him how bad things
were.

God thought, then he said, "Don't bother your heads.
They don't call me God for nothing. I will give you one well
for everyone to use."

The animals thanked God. They told him he was very
considerate. God said, "But you'll have to take good care of
my well. One of you will have to be caretaker. He will stay by
the well at all times to see that no one abuses it or makes it
dirty."

Mabouya, the ground lizard spoke up saying, "I will be the
caretaker."

God looked at all the animals. He said at last, "Mabouya,
the lizard, looks like the best caretaker. Therefore, I appoint
him. He will be the watchman. The well is over there in the
mango grove."

The animals went away. The lizard went directly to the
well. When the other animals began to come back for water,

Mabouya challenged them. First the cow came to drink. The lizard sang out in a deep voice:

> "Who is it? Who is it?
> Who is walking in my grove?"

The cow replied:

> "It is I, the cow,
> I am coming for water."

And the lizard called back:

> "Go away! This is God's grove,
> And the well is dry."

So the cow went away and suffered from thirst.
Then the horse came and the lizard challenged him, saying:

> "Who is it? Who is it?
> Who is walking in my grove?"

The horse answered:

> "It is I, the horse,
> I am coming for water."

And the lizard called back:

> "Go away! This is God's grove,
> And the well is dry."

So the horse went away and he too suffered from thirst.
Each animal came to the well and the lizard challenged all of them in the same way, saying:

> "Go away! This is God's grove,
> And the well is dry."

So the animals went away and suffered much because they had no water to drink.

When God saw all the suffering going on, he said, "I gave the animals a well to drink from, but they are all dying of thirst. What is the matter?" And he himself went to the well. When the lizard heard his footsteps, he called out:

> "Who is it? Who is it?
> Who is walking in my grove?"

God answered:

> "It is I, Papa God.
> I am coming for water."

And the lizard said:

> "Go away, Papa God.
> The well is dry."

God was very angry. He said once more:

> "It is I, Papa God.
> I am coming for water."

And the lizard called back to him again:

> "Go away, Papa God.
> The well is dry."

God said no more to the lizard. He sent for the animals to come to the well. He said, "You came to me because you were thirsty and I gave you a well. I made Mabouya the caretaker. But he gave no thought to the suffering creatures all around him. If a man has a banana tree in his garden, it is his. If a man has a cotton tree in his garden, it is his. But if a man has a well in his garden, only the hole in the ground belongs to him. The water is God's and belongs to all creatures. Because Mabouya, the lizard, became drunk with conceit, he is no longer the caretaker. Henceforth, he must drink his water from puddles wherever the rain falls. The new caretaker will be the frog. The frog will not say, 'Go away, the well is dry.' He will say, 'This is God's well; this is God's well'."

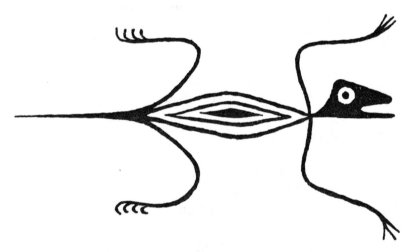

And the lizard called back to him, "Go away, Papa God."

So the animals drank at the well, while Mabouya, the lizard, went away from it and drank rain water wherever he could find it. The frog is now the caretaker. And all night he calls out:

> "This is God's well!
> This is God's well!
> This is God's well!"

And it is a saying among the people:

> "The hole in the ground is yours,
> The water is God's."

(This story was taken from *The Piece of Fire and Other Haitian Tales,* ©
1964 by Harold Courlander. Reprinted by permission of Harcourt, Brace
and Jovanovich, Inc., New York. Story came originally from West
Africa.)

17
NIGHT AND DAY
AND
THE SEASONS
(From the Western Mountains
of Canada)

How can two people reach an agreement when
their wishes are completely opposite?

O NE TIME GRIZZLY BEAR MET COYOTE and said, "I am the
greatest magician in the world! When I wish a thing
to be so, it has to be so."

Coyote looked doubtful.

"Well, then, I'll show you," said Grizzly. "Now, I don't
like light. I like darkness. I want darkness all the time. I
intend to make it so!"

Coyote answered, "No, you must not do that. I like it *light*
all the time! Besides, the people on the earth could not live if
it were dark all the time."

"That doesn't matter to me," growled Grizzly. "I want it
my way. Dark all the time!"

"No, you must not!" exclaimed Coyote. "I won't let you!"

"I can, and I will," declared Grizzly.

He began to dance and sing, "Darkness, darkness, darkness! Let it always be darkness!"

But then Coyote began to dance around Grizzly, and to
sing. "Light, light, light, may it always be light!" he sang.

Growled Grizzly, "I want it my way. Dark all the time."

For a long, long time, they danced and sang. Sometimes Grizzly danced around Coyote and the world was dark. Then Coyote would dance around Grizzly and the world would be light again. For a long time, they struggled to see which would win out completely, but neither one succeeded.

At last, Grizzly grew tired of all the dancing and said, "All right, then, let there be *half* darkness and *half* light."

"I agree to that," said Coyote. "From this time on, it shall be light from the time the sun rises until it sets. The rest of the time, it will be dark."

This plan seemed good to the people too and they were happy. For a while, things went along peacefully. But then Grizzly began to be dissatisfied again.

"The problem is that the winter is too short!" he said to Coyote. "I want the winter to have many more months. Let there be the same number of months for winter as there are feathers in the tail of a blue grouse!"

Coyote counted the feathers and found that there were twenty-two.

"No, no!" he exclaimed. "Twenty-two months of winter are too many. That will never do. The people could not endure such a long winter. They would all die. Let it be half that number!"

"No, no," exclaimed Grizzly. "I must have the long, long winter!"

"Would you agree to have as many months in the year as there are feathers in the tail of a red-winged flicker?" asked Coyote.

Grizzly thought there were many feathers in the tail of a flicker, so he said that would be all right. But he wanted them all to be winter.

"No, that's too many," Coyote insisted. "But we can compromise. Would you agree that half the number of feathers in the tail of the red-winged flicker would be winter, and half would be summer?"

Grizzly thought that over and said he thought that he could accept that.

"All right, then," said Coyote. "Half of the flicker's tail feathers will tell the number of months in which it may snow. The other half will tell the number in which it will be warm and sunny. Agreed?"

Grizzly hesitated but finally agreed. It wasn't exactly as he wanted it, but he thought there would be a good many months anyway for winter.

Together they counted the feathers in the flicker's tail. There were only twelve! Grizzly was disappointed and angry, but it was too late to change. The agreement had already been made.

Coyote said then, "All right. From this time on, there will be six months in which it will be cold. There will be six other months that will be warm and sunny."

Thus Coyote was a friend to the people. He saved them from having cold and darkness all the year around. He gave them day, too, along with night, and the seasons as they are now.

Adapted from James A. Teit "The Shusway," in *Memoirs of the American Museum of Natural History,* Vol. 4, "Ethnology and Archaeology of Southern British Columbia and Washington," pp. 625-626 (Leiden, Holland, and New York, American Museum of Natural History, 1900-1908). Reprint permission granted by American Museum of Natural History.

Stories About
War and Peace

18

TWO SELFISH KINGS
(From the Buddhists)

What is worth fighting for?

T WO KINGS HAD FOR MANY MONTHS been quarreling over a small piece of land. There a high bank had been made to stop a river from flooding the fields around it. "This bank belongs to my country," said one of the kings.

"No," said the other king. "This bank belongs to *my* country."

The more they talked, the angrier the kings became. Finally, since they could not agree peaceably, they decided to fight the matter out. Each one called his army to prepare for battle. Each king planned to be ready the next day to lead his army forth to fight the other king and *his* army.

Buddha heard that the two kings were planning to fight each other. He sent a messenger to each one saying, "Before you go to war, will you please allow me to hear your complaints? Perhaps I may help you to find some other way of settling your quarrel."

Neither king was very happy about meeting Buddha. Still they both consented and came to the house of the teacher. There the three men sat down together to talk the whole matter over.

Buddha began, in his gentle way, to ask the kings certain questions. First he would put his question to one king and then he would ask the same question of the other king. "Why do you say that the bank belongs to your kingdom?" he asked. "Of what use is the bank to you if it does belong to you? What will you do with it?"

The more they talked, the angrier the kings became.

When Buddha thought he understood the reasons for their quarrel, he asked another question, first of one, then of the other. "If you go to battle over this bank of earth, will not many of your soldiers be killed? May not you yourselves even lose your lives?"

"That is true," the kings admitted. "Many will be killed. But what else can we do?"

"Which is worth more: a bank of earth, or the lives of your men, or your own lives?" asked Buddha.

"Of course the lives of our men are worth far more than a bank of earth." Both kings agreed on that.

Buddha had one more question still to ask. "Which would take more money: to build another bank or to put back the lives of men once dead?"

"The lives of men cannot be brought back with all the money in the world," said the kings. "The lives of men are priceless."

"Are you then going to risk what is so precious that no money can ever buy it back, in order to have a small piece of ground that is like the ground on a thousand other hills?"

As the two kings talked and listened, they began to lose their angry feelings and to work out a peaceable agreement. In the end they did not go to war, and for many years the people of the two countries lived side by side in peace.

(This story is taken from *The Gospel of Buddha,* by Paul Carus and published by Open Court Publishing Co., Chicago, 1915.) Reprint permission granted by Open Court Publishing Company.

19

THE TWO SISTERS

(From the Capilanos of North America)

How can war be changed into peace?

M ANY THOUSANDS OF YEARS AGO a great Tyee or tribal chief had two daughters who grew to womanhood at the same springtime. This was when the first great run of salmon thronged the rivers and the ollallie bushes were heavy with blossoms. The two daughters were young and very beautiful. Their father, the great Tyee, prepared to make such a feast as the Coast had never seen. There were to be days and days of rejoicing. The people were to come from far places and were to bring gifts and to receive gifts of great value from the Chief. Hospitality was to reign as long as feet could dance and lips could laugh and mouths could enjoy the Chief's fish, game, and ollallies.

The only shadow on the joy of it all was *war*. It happened that the tribe of the Great Tyee was at war with the Upper Coast Indians. They lived in the north, near what is called by the White man the Port of Prince Rupers. Great war canoes slipped along the entire coast; war parties paddled up and down; war songs broke the silences of the nights. Hatred, vengeance, strife, and horror festered everywhere like sores on the surface of the earth.

But the great Tyee, after warring for weeks, turned and laughed at the battle and the bloodshed. He had been victor in every encounter so far. He could well afford to leave the strife for a week to feast in his daughters' honor. No enemy was to come between him and the traditions of his race and household! He turned insultingly deaf ears to the war cries.

104

He ignored with arrogant indifference the paddle dips that encroached within his own coast waters. He prepared, as a great Tyee should, to entertain his tribesmen royally in honor of his twin daughters.

But then, seven suns before the great feast, these two maidens came before their father, hand clasped in hand. "Oh, our father," they said, "may we speak?"

"Speak then, my daughters," he answered, "my girls with the eyes of April and the hearts of June!"

"Some day, oh, our father," said the one, "we may each mother a man-child who may grow to be just such a powerful Tyee as you are. For this that may some day be ours, we have come to crave a favor from you, oh, our father!"

"It is your privilege at this celebration to receive any favor your hearts may wish," he replied graciously, placing his fingers beneath their chins. "The favor is yours before you ask it, my daughters."

"Will you, for our sakes, invite the great northern hostile tribe to our feast?" the second one asked.

"To a peaceful feast, a feast in honor of woman?" he exclaimed, not believing his ears.

"So we would desire it," they answered.

"Well, then, so it shall be," he agreed. "I can deny you nothing on this day. Some time you may bear sons to bless this peace you have asked, and to bless their mothers' sire for granting it!"

Then he turned to all the young men of the tribe and commanded them, "Build fires at sunset on all the coast headlands. Build fires of welcome. Man your canoes. Face the north, greet the enemy, and tell them that the Tyee of the Capilanos asks that they join him for a great feast in honor of his two daughters. By this, pledge to them our friendship."

When the northern tribes heard this invitation and this pledge, they flocked down the coast to the feast of the Great

Peace. They brought grain and fish, gold and white stone beads, baskets and carved ladles. They brought wonderful woven blankets to lay at the feet of their new friend, the great Tyee.

The Tyee in turn gave such a potlatch that never was another given to equal it. Those were long glad days of joyousness, long pleasurable nights of dancing and campfires and vast quantities of food. The war canoes were emptied of their deadly weapons and filled with the daily catch of salmon. The hostile war songs ceased. In their place were heard

In the cup of his hand he lifted the two daughters and set them forever in a high place.

the soft shuffle of dancing feet, the singing voices of women, the play games of the children of two powerful tribes which had been until now ancient enemies. A great and lasting brotherhood was sealed between them. Their war songs ended forever.

Then the great Tyee of all men (the Great Spirit) smiled on his Indian children. "I will make these young-eyed maidens immortal," he said. "They have given birth to two offspring, Peace and Brotherhood, greater than any great Tyee that ever ruled his tribe."

In the cup of his hand he lifted the two daughters and set them forever in a high place. On the mountain crest the chief's daughters may still be seen. Sometimes they are wrapped in clouds, or sometimes capped with snow. Sometimes they are glorified in the purple and blue and azure of the changing sunlit sky. There they have stood for thousands of years, and there they will stand for thousands of years to come, guarding the peace of the Pacific coast and the quiet of the Capilano Canyon.

(This story was taken from *Legends of Vancouver,* by Emily Pauline Johnson, published by Saturday Sunset Press, Vancouver, B.C., 2nd ed. G. S. Forsyth, Vancouver, 1912.)

20

KRISHNA, CHAMPION OF THE OPPRESSED

(From the Hindus)

When, if ever, is it right to go to war?

ACCORDING TO A HINDU STORY, long ago there came a time when the people became jealous and deceitful, and the leaders oppressive. Priests became insincere and some stole the gifts brought to the gods. Kings were tyrannical. Tribes and nations were continually warring one against another.

Then Brahman, the Eternal One, decided to give mankind a special helper, a human Savior who would live among men and protect and guide them and teach them the way to live. And so it happened that one day a divine child was born. At his birth, angels appeared, singing praises. They bowed down before him and named him Krishna, the Savior of Mankind, the incarnation of the Eternal Brahman.

Now Krishna of course was a human being as well as a god. He was born in India where at that time everyone belonged to a "caste." His was the Warrior caste, which meant that his *dharma* or destiny must be fulfilled in war and struggle.

But as a child Krishna did not seem to be a warlike person. He lived happily with other children, wandering with them over the fields and woods, and helping to tend the cows. He

108

learned to play the flute, and often played it while his young friends danced together. A strong boy, he soon became a favorite among his friends, perhaps because he always seemed to use his strength to protect the weak. Many tales have been told of Krishna's gallant and miraculous deeds during his youth. Always these were done in order to protect some innocent sufferer, or to save some person or animal in trouble.

As Krishna grew older, he left his happy life as a cowherd, became a student of the sacred books, and gave himself to a life of simple living and fasting. His teacher was amazed at his brilliance and devotion.

After finishing his studies, Krishna became the champion of one tribe or another which had been unjustly treated. Always his championship was of the weak against the strong and the evil. If happiness were to be spread among all the people, cruelty had to be destroyed even if war must be waged to achieve this. Thus Krishna, born into the Warrior caste, was true to his *dharma*.

As the years passed, the warring groups in India grew stronger and larger and the battles became fiercer until India became divided into two warring nations. One nation was ruled by the evil king, Duryodhana; the other, by the good king, Yudisthira, long remembered for his justice and goodwill. Finally, the selfish and ambitious King Duryodhana banished the good King Yudisthira and his people into exile and refused to allow even five villages to be shared with them.

After Yudisthira had tried unsuccessfully for thirteen years to settle the matter without a major battle, preparations were begun for an all-out war between the armies of the two kings. Both sides came to Krishna asking for his help. Duryodhana, the evil king, asked Krishna for armies. Arjuna, the brother of the good King Yudisthira, asked not for armies but for Krishna alone, saying "Friendship is the strongest weapon in the world. I want *you* for my charioteer." Both kings were granted their wishes, and Duryodhana chuckled at Arjuna's foolishness.

Not long after, in the red dawning of the morning, the two great armies faced each other on the sandy plains of Kurukshetra. The evil king was in his chariot at the head of one great army, now even larger than before. Arjuna, brother of the good king, was in his chariot at the head of the other army. But with Arjuna stood the god Krishna as charioteer.

Arjuna looked about and his heart grew faint, for he saw the faces of fathers and grandfathers, teachers, uncles, sons, brothers, grandsons, and friends. He spoke despairingly to Krishna:

"O Krishna, Krishna! Now that I look on all my own kinsmen, arrayed for battle, my limbs have become weak, my mouth, is parching, my body trembles, my hair stands upright, my skin seems to be burning! My bow slips from my hand and my brain is whirling round and round. What can I hope for from this killing of kinsmen? What do I want with victory and empire?"

> "Krishna, hearing the prayers of all men,
> Tell me how we can hope to be happy
> Slaying the sons of Dritarashtra?
> Evil they may be, worst of the wicked,
> Yet if we kill them, *our* sin is greater.

*　　*　　*　　*　　*　　*　　*

> "What is the crime I am planning, O Krishna?
> Murder most hateful, murder of brothers!
> Am I indeed so greedy for greatness?
> Rather let the evil children come with their weapons
> Against me in battle!
> I shall not struggle, I shall not strike them.
> Now let them kill me, that will be better."

Having spoken so feelingly, Arjuna threw aside his arrows and his bow. He stood as if already mortally wounded, his heart torn with sorrow.

Krishna was silent for a while. Arjuna tried once more to speak. "Which is worst," he cried out again, "to win this war, or to lose it? I scarcely know. My mind gropes about in darkness. I cannot see where my duty lies. Krishna, I beg you to tell me frankly and clearly what I ought to do. I am your disciple. I have put myself into your hands. Show me the way."

Krishna then answered: "Your words are wise, Arjuna, but your sorrow is for nothing. The truly wise person mourns neither for the living nor for the dead. Bodies are said to die, but THAT which *possesses* the body is eternal. It cannot be limited or destroyed. The real life within each one cannot be wounded by weapons, nor burned by fire, nor dried by the wind, nor wet by water. It is deathless and birthless. It is indestructible. Therefore, never mourn for anyone.

"And besides, Arjuna, you were born in the warring caste. Fighting to protect, fighting to save others from oppression, is your duty. If you turn aside from this righteous way, you will be a sinner.

"Die, Arjuna, and you win Nirvana. Conquer and you enjoy the earth. Stand up now, and resolve to fight. Realize that pleasure and pain, gain and loss, victory and defeat are one and the same; then go into battle."

So Arjuna, the disciple of Krishna, rose and obeyed. A conch was blown and the blare of a thousand conches responded. Arrows shot through the air like meteors; the sun itself was shrouded in the dust of the battle. Horses leaped; men ran at each other with swords. Hundreds, even thousands, were wounded or slain.

With each new dawn, the battle was begun afresh, day after day for eighteen days. Finally, the evil King Duryodhana was slain, and Arjuna and Yudisthira were the victors.

In the early dawn after the battle, the plain was grim with

So Arjuna, the disciple of Krishna, rose and obeyed.

the bloody burden of thousands of dead. It was a weary sight for miles around. Weeping wives searched for the bodies of their lost husbands. Mothers mourned over their dead sons. An old grandmother sat on the ground and wept. "O shame on prowess!" she cried. "Shame on courage! Shame on *war* that leaves weeping women to bear the burden of grief!"

In spite of all this, because of the terrible war and the courageous victory of Arjuna, there was finally peace in the land. Yudisthira was crowned king of both nations. He reigned as undisputed ruler of all India for thirty-six years and in his time there was justice throughout the kingdom. The people saw in Yudisthira the ideals which Lord Krishna had taught them to attain.

"He did not hate any living creature.
He was friendly and compassionate to all,
He freed himself of the delusion of "Me" and "Mine,"
He accepted pleasure and pain with tranquility,
He was forgiving, ever contented, self-controlled,
He was neither vain nor anxious about the result of his
    actions."

(Based on extracts from an unpublished manuscript, "India's Story of Krishna," by Sophia Lyon Fahs. This was based in turn on *Bhagavad Gita: The Song of God,* translated by Swami Prabhavananda and Christopher Isherwood (Hollywood, California: Vedanta Society of Southern California, latest edition 1972). Extracts are quoted with the permission of the Vedanta Society of Southern California.)

Stories About Seeking Riches

21

THE KING WITH THE GOLDEN TOUCH

(From Greece)

What happens when one is too eager for gold?

KING MIDAS ONCE DID A GREAT FAVOR for Bacchus, the god of wine. In return, Bacchus offered to grant Midas one wish—no matter what it might be.

Now Midas had come to be king the hard way and he knew what it meant to be poor. Also, he had found that if one has money it is possible to buy almost everything one wants, including power.

"The more gold one has, the more powerful one can be," Midas said to himself. "And surely it is good to be powerful." To the god Bacchus he said, "I wish that I could change anything into gold simply by touching it!"

"That isn't a wise wish, my friend!" Bacchus exclaimed. "Are you sure it is what you want?"

Midas was perfectly sure, so Bacchus with some reluctance granted the wish. Scarcely believing the god, Midas at once began to try out his new power by plucking a twig of oak from a branch overhead. The branch became gold in his hand. He rubbed his eyes in astonishment.

He picked up a stone. It changed to gold.

He touched a sod of earth. It changed to gold!

He picked an apple from a tree nearby. The apple changed

115

to shining gold!

Midas' joy knew no bounds. He rushed home, ordered his servants to prepare a feast, and invited all his friends to come. In fact, he was so eager to begin celebrating his good fortune that he began tasting the food as it appeared on the table.

He picked up a piece of bread. It hardened in his hand.

He took a drink of wine. The cup changed to gold and the wine flowed down his throat like melted gold.

He tried to eat the bread. It was too hard to bite!

Midas realized that he could no longer eat anything! He would starve!

"I must get *rid* of this power!" he cried. "It will ruin me!"

He raised his arms above his head and then realized that his sleeves were all shining now because his clothing had changed to gold.

In desperation, Midas rushed out into the garden where he saw his own little daughter running toward him. She was in his arms before he could stop her. Alas, as he embraced her, Midas felt the child hardening into gold!

"Dear Bacchus!" he cried. "Pray, take back the gift. You were right. It was not a wise wish that I made. I do *not* want gold. I want only my child. And to be like other people. That is all!"

Bacchus, being his friend, heard the prayer.

"You have discovered the truth about riches sooner than many people," he said. "And you have learned the lesson. Go now to the river. Trace the stream to its fountainhead, then plunge in your head and body and wash away your fault and its punishment!"

Midas did as he was told. Scarcely had he touched the waters before the gold-creating power passed from him. The river sands became changed into gold. When he returned to his home, he rejoiced to find his little daughter exactly as she had been before.

Thenceforth, Midas, hating wealth and splendor, dwelt in the country, a simple, happy farmer. He no longer had wealth and power, but he had what he wanted more—the right to be like other men.

The sands of the river remain gold to this day!

(Adapted from *Bulfinch's Mythology: The Age of Fable,* New York: Thos. Y. Crowell, Publishers, 1970.) Reprint permission granted by Harper & Row, Publishers, Inc.

"I must get rid of this power!" he cried. "It will ruin me!"

22

THE RICH
YOUNG MAN

(From the Early Christians)

How should riches be used?

M ANY PEOPLE CAME TO JESUS with questions—all kinds of questions. Some were rich, some poor; some old, some young. Jesus especially enjoyed the children, but he accepted them all and advised them. Of course, people were not always pleased with what he had to say. One of these was a well-to-do young man belonging to the ruling class in Israel. He admired Jesus and Jesus liked him, too.

"Good Master," the young man said, "What must I do if I want to live forever?"

"You must not call me good," Jesus said. "Only God is good. But your question is worth thinking about. First of all, you probably know the commandments which God gave to Moses so long ago—do not lie, do not steal, do not kill, honor your father and mother, and all the others."

"Oh, yes," the young man said. "I know them all and I've kept them all, too, ever since I was a small boy."

Jesus looked at the young man for a long time and loved him!

"You have done well," he said. "But there is one thing missing. What you must do now is to sell everything you own and give the money to poor people who have nothing."

"Everything?" exclaimed the young man.

"Everything!" Jesus declared. "You will have plenty of

riches later on. Give up all your possessions now and come, follow me!"

The young man's heart sank. He was a very *rich* man! After a moment, he turned slowly away, without saying a word.

Jesus waited until he was out of sight before speaking to his disciples.

"You see how hard it is for a wealthy person!" he said. If you have much, you must give much. It is very hard, but it is not impossible. It all depends on the kind of treasure a person's heart is set on. Where one's treasure is, there is one's heart also. Of course, that young man may yet decide to come with us. But truly, it is easier for a camel to go through the eye of a needle than for a rich man to get into heaven!"

"He seemed like a good man," John observed. "If he can't make it, can anybody of his rank get to heaven?"

"God can bring it about," Jesus said. "Perhaps this man will some time come with us."

After a moment he turned slowly away without saying a word.

"Well, we disciples hadn't so much to begin with, but we have given it all up to be your followers," Peter said, and Jesus answered him quickly. "I can tell you this," he said. "There is no one who has given up home, or even family, for the sake of God, who will not be repaid many times in this life and in the life to come."

(There is a story—perhaps it is true—that after Jesus was condemned to death by the Sanhedrin and was ordered to carry his own cross to the place where he would be crucified, this very same young man came out of the crowd and took the load from Jesus. Perhaps the rich young ruler did find his way into the kingdom!)

(Retold from the *Holy Bible: New Testament*. Matthew Chapter 19: 16-24. Mark Chapter 10:17-22. Luke Chapter 18:18-30.)

23
THE MAGIC PILLOW
(From Ancient China)

What are some of the problems wealth may bring?

A TAOIST PRIEST WHO HAD ACQUIRED the magic of the Immortals was traveling one time on the road and stopped at an inn. As he was sitting there and resting with his back against his bag, he was joined in a pleasant conversation by a young man named Lu Sheng. The man wore a short coat, rode a black colt, and appeared to be a student, laboring in the fields while he waited for the time of his examinations. He had stopped at the inn on his way to work.

After a while, Lu Sheng suddenly sighed as he looked at his shabby clothes. "It is because fate is against me that I am such a failure in life!" he said.

"Why do you say that?" asked the priest. "As far as I can see, you suffer from nothing and appear to enjoy the best of health."

"But this is mere existence," Lu Sheng protested. "I do not call it life!"

"What do you call life?" asked the priest.

"A man ought to achieve great things and make a name for himself. He should be a general, or a great minister at court. He should cause his clan to prosper and his own family to be rich. These are the things that make for life as I see it," Lu Sheng sighed. "I used to think I could have them all, but now alas I will probably never do any better than labor in the fields."

After he finished speaking, Lu Sheng felt a sudden drowsiness, which may have been caused by the steam from the mil-

121

let which the innkeeper was cooking. All was quiet.

At that moment, the priest reached into his bag, took out a pillow, and gave it to the young man, saying, "Rest your head on this pillow. It will help you to fulfill your wishes!"

Suddenly, Lu Sheng seemed to be back in his own home and strange things began to happen! His wealth began to increase. The number of luxuries with which he surrounded himself multiplied day by day. A year passed and he joined the court.

There followed one promotion after another. He became a governor of the metropolitan district, then a governor general, and finally he was president of the Board of Revenue. No name carried more prestige.

But all this incurred the intense and bitter jealousy of the other ministers at court. Finally, as a result of repeated slanderous attacks, Lu Sheng was banished to a far away provincial post.

Three miserable years passed before he was recalled to court and became counselor to the emperor. But again he fell victim to the jealousy and suspicions of his colleagues. This time they charge him with conspiring to overthrow the dynasty and he was thrown into prison.

When they came to arrest him, he was stricken with terror and cried, "Back in my homeland we have good land! Why should I have sought rank and title which in the end have brought only calamity? Alas, it is now too late to wish that I could ride back and forth on the country road as I once did, wearing my plain hempen coat!"

He drew his sword to kill himself, but was restrained from doing so. Then it happened that his innocence was determined. He was finally returned to the Imperial Council with the title of Duke.

So he lived for more than fifty years. During that time he was twice punished by being banished to the frontier wilds. Each time he was recalled to court, vindicated, and given greater honors than before.

He became extravagant and addicted to pleasures. His inner apartments were filled with dancers and beautiful women. Innumerable were the gifts of fertile lands, mansions, fleet horses, and treasures that the Emperor bestowed upon him.

When advanced age made him wish to retire from court life, his request was refused. At last he fell ill and nothing was left undone that eminent physicians could do. But all was in vain. He became worse until one night he died!

At this very moment, Lu Sheng awoke with a start. He found himself lying as before in the roadside inn, with the priest sitting by his side. The millet was still cooking.

I now know at last the way of honor and disgrace and the meaning of

"Could it be that I have been dreaming all this while?" Lu Sheng asked, rising to his feet.

"You have been asleep," the priest replied. "But life as you would have it is exactly as you have dreamed it."

For a long time Lu Sheng reflected in silence. At last, he said, "I now know at last the way of honor and disgrace, and the meaning of poverty and fortune, and the recurring way of gain and loss. I owe all this kindness to you, good priest. Since you have thus deigned to instruct me in the vanity of ambition, dare I refuse to profit thereby?"

With this, he bowed profoundly to the priest, and went away.

(Adapted and reprinted from *Traditional Chinese Tales,* with permission of the translator Chi-Chen Wang, 21 Claremong Ave., N.Y., N.Y. 10027. Copyrighted 1944 by Columbia University Press, paperback edition, Greenwood Press, 1976, pp. 20-23.)

24
BLOOD OF
THE POOR

(From Italy)

When, if ever, should donations for
good causes be refused?

H ERE IS THE STORY of St. Ignatius of Sardinia, a Capuchin monk, canonized in 1951:

Ignatius used to go out from his monastery with a sack to beg from the people of the town. But he would never go up to a certain merchant who was known to have built his fortune by defrauding the poor. Franchino, the merchant, a very rich man, fumed every time Ignatius passed his door without begging. However, his concern was not the loss of opportunity to give alms, but the fear of what people would think! He complained at the monk's residence, whereupon the Father Guardian there ordered Ignatius to be sure to beg from the merchant the next time he went out.

"Very well," said Ignatius. "If you wish it, Father, I will go to the merchant, but I am unwilling to ask him for alms!"

The wealthy merchant received Ignatius with much flattery and, without being asked, gave him generous alms. He also asked the monk to come again in the future. But hardly had Ignatius left the rich man's house, with his sack on his shoulder, than some drops of blood began coming from the sack. They trickled down the merchant's doorstep and down through the street, all the way back to the monastery. Everywhere Ignatius went with his sack, a trickle of blood followed him.

When he arrived at the monastery, Ignatius laid the sack at the Father Guardian's feet.

"What is this?" gasped the Guardian.

"This," said Ignatius, "is the blood of the poor!"

Quoted from a column by Dorothy Day, "Poverty and Precarity," in *The Catholic Worker,* May, 1952, reprinted, September 1979.

Everywhere Ignatius went with his sack.

Stories About What Is "Men's Work" and What Is "Women's Work"

25
WHEN FIRST MAN AND FIRST WOMAN QUARRELED

(From the Navajos of North America)

What is necessary if men and women
are to get along together?

FIRST MAN WAS THE CHIEF of all the people in the world. He was a great hunter and enjoyed bringing home the animals he had killed in the hunt. First Woman did the cooking. In fact she cooked so well that they both ate more than they needed to, and First Woman grew very fat. First Man stayed thin because he walked through the woods all day long hunting. First Woman stayed at home, and did less active things like planting and tending the garden, grinding corn, cooking, and making clothing, pottery, and baskets.

One day First Man came in dragging a fine fat deer behind him.

"This ought to be enough to last a long time!" he said. "I must say I'm a good provider!"

First Woman agreed. "But," she said, "I'm a good cook, too!"

First Man didn't appear to pay much attention to that.

"You do very well," she went on then. "But it's only because I'm such a good wife to you!"

First Man turned and looked at her.

"What's that you said?" he demanded. "What makes you think I do well *only* because you're such a good wife? What does that have to do with it?"

"I cook and make clothing and pottery—and do some *other* things that you couldn't get along without!'' she said.

"I brought home that deer today," he insisted. "You couldn't have cooked it if I hadn't killed it."

"And you wouldn't have killed it if it hadn't been for all the things *I* do!" she answered him. "If I weren't such a good wife to you, you couldn't get along at all. If you didn't have me to care for you and your children, to love you in the day time, and to sleep with you at night, you would be very unhappy!"

"Then maybe all you women think you can get along without the men!" he exclaimed.

"Of course we could!" she answered. "We women are the ones who till the fields and gather food. We can live on the produce of our fields, and the seeds and fruits we collect. We don't need the men. It's *you* who couldn't get along without *us*!"

First Man became more and more angry with every word she said, until at last, infuriated, he jumped across the fire and went to bed. First Woman slept on the other side of the fire, and all night long they stayed apart.

Next morning First Man went out early and called aloud to the people.

"Come here, all you *men*," he said. "I wish to speak to you. But let the women stay behind. I don't wish even to *see* them."

Soon all the men were gathered near him, and he told them what had happened.

"She said I wouldn't bring home the deer except for what *she* does!" he exclaimed. "She believes the women could live without us!"

The men all growled and shook their heads.

"Well, they can't!" another muttered. "We could do better without them!"

"Silly women!" another muttered. "We could do better without them!"

"All right then," First Man said. "Let's see if they can hunt game and till the fields without our help. Let's see what kind of a living they can make by themselves. Let's *leave* them! We'll cross the stream and when we're on the other side we'll keep the raft, so they can't get over!"

"We'll show them!" they all shouted.

So they all gathered at the side of the river, and crossed over to the other side on the raft, taking along with them their stone axes and farm implements and almost everything they had made. They didn't leave much behind, but the women pretended not even to notice. They set about fixing up the place without the men.

As soon as they had crossed the river, some of the men went out hunting, and some set to work chopping down willows and building huts. In four days they had made shelters for all the men.

"See!" they said to each other. "We're doing just fine without the women, poor things! I wonder what they're doing without us!"

At first the women had a great deal of food, and they feasted and sang and had a merry time. They often came down to the bank of the river, and called across to the men, taunting and teasing them.

That year the men prepared a few small fields and raised a little corn, but they were not good gardeners and also did not have enough seedlings. As a result they found they did not have enough to eat. The next year they did better, and of course they lived a good deal by hunting. But they were not good cooks like the women.

Meanwhile the women planted seeds, but the weather that

first year was not very good for growing, so like the men, they had a poor crop. They missed the meat the men brought home, too, and began to be very hungry.

There were other things they missed too—both the men and the women—but they tried not to think of those things.

That first year several babies were born, and whenever the baby was a boy it was sent over to where the men were. The girl babies stayed with their mothers.

The second year there were no more babies born. Since this continued during the third and fourth years, First Man began to worry about what might happen in the future. It looked as though eventually all the people might die out.

"Maybe we ought to go back," he said to some of the others. "We don't want our people to disappear."

"That's right," another of the men said. "And the women probably need some help."

"I hate to think of my wife getting thin without any meat," another said.

Finally First Man sent a man to the shore to call across the stream and find out if First Woman was still there. When she came to the bank First Man called to her.

"Do you still think you can live alone?" he asked.

She waited a long time, and then said "No, to tell the truth, we miss our husbands!"

That touched the heart of First Man. "To tell the truth, we miss our wives too!" he said.

Then he turned to the other men and asked, "Shall we take them back again?"

They all agreed that they should.

"They won't be so hard to get along with after this!" they said to each other.

So the men rowed across the river and brought the women back with them to the men's camp which by this time was quite well built, and had fields around it.

The women agreed that the men had done a good job

learning to plant seed and raise crops, whereas they, the women, never had learned how to kill deer and large game. Also the women's shelters had been neglected and become shaky during those four years.

So the women were glad to join the men again, and the men were glad to have them back.

(Adapted from *Navajo Legends,* by Washington Matthews. Published for the American Folk Lore Society by Houghton, Mifflin and Company of Boston and New York, 1897.)

The women were glad to join the men again, and the men were glad to have them back.

26
THE DETERMINED DAUGHTER

(From Ancient China)

**What must women do if they are to
influence major policy decisions?**

T HE CHINESE PEOPLE TRADITIONALLY PLACED great
emphasis upon the devotion of children to their parents,
particularly on the responsibility of the son to his father and
mother. Girls and young women were not expected to be of
much worth, and although age brought eminence and the
aged grandmother was deeply venerated, she had no great
importance as a young person. Very few girls were taught to
read and write, and none had leadership in the family. It was
always a great disappointment when a baby turned out to be
a girl instead of a boy. The following story is exceptional
because a young girl is represented as a scholar, a diplomat,
and a savior.

About the year 150 B.C., there lived in China a man named
Schwen. He was placed in charge of all the country's granaries by the Emperor himself. This was an important posi-
tion, and Schwen was a good and just man. He also had
some knowledge of medicine. He used his knowledge to help
the poor rather than the rich. This, of course, made him
beloved by the peasants, but it angered the people of higher
rank.

Schwen's rich neighbors became more and more jealous.

133

Finally they began to plot against him. They told the court officials that Schwen was using his power to sell grain illegally in order to profit himself at the expense of the people. (The tale-bearers pretended to be very sorry about all this!)

Their wicked purpose seemed to be achieved when word came that the Emperor was sending for Schwen to come to the capital city to answer the charges. Of course, with that summons came the threat of terrible punishment if he could not prove himself innocent. He might even have his nose cut off, or both his heels, or he might be branded on the forehead.

Schwen could not think who might have spread the lies. He tried to find friends to defend him but, alas, his friends were only the poor. He knew their word would not be believed against the word of the rich people who were accusing him. With despair in his heart, he prepared to obey the imperial summons and to go to the city alone because he had no son to go with him or to defend him.

Now, although heaven had not blessed Schwen with a son, he was fortunate to have a very loving and loyal daughter. Ti Tuan was the youngest of three sisters, but she was also the wisest and kindest and the one most concerned about her father's trouble. After thinking it all over, she went to her father and begged to be allowed to travel with him to the Emperor.

At first, he flatly refused to permit such a thing.

"The journey is long and very trying," he told her. "It's hard and dangerous. Besides, of what use could you possibly be? You are only a girl, my dear. You are not, alas, a son!"

"Indeed, I wish I were a son," Ti Tuan said humbly. "But even if I am only a girl, I am not so helpless as you think. Please let me go with you and help you — as a son might do."

Well, Schwen thought, she was a strong, courageous and loving girl — and it *would* be pleasant to have her company.

At last, he agreed to let her go with him.

Ti Tuan was delighted and began at once to make her preparations. The first thing she did was to write, with great care, a letter stating all that her father had done to help the poor people of his district and how well he looked after the granaries.

At last he agreed to let her go with him.

"How fortunate that my father allowed me to learn to write!" she said to herself as she put her sentences down on paper. After the letter was finished, she read it over with satisfaction, for it was indeed a good one, as she well knew. It even included a suggestion to the Emperor that he look carefully into the whole matter. Also that he call witnesses among the poor who could testify to her father's honesty. It was a clear statement, she thought, which ought to influence his majesty.

The journey to the capital was long and weary. Both father and daughter were exhausted when they at last sighted the city where the Emperor held his court. But alas, their troubles were not over. They had no sooner arrived at the gate to the palace than Schwen was arrested and thrown into prison. (His enemies had already heard of his coming and were ready for him!) Ti Tuan had to go alone to find lodging in a nearby inn where she lay awake all night long.

"I have truth for my weapon," she kept telling herself. "Truth must conquer, even if I am only a woman."

But her father's enemies were at work! Knowing that Ti Tuan had come along to defend him, they had arranged with the gatekeeper at the palace to refuse her admission. For several days, she was kept waiting. Every morning early she would go to seek audience with the Emperor, but every morning the guard there stood in the way.

Now Ti Tuan possessed one large jewel of great value which she had brought along to sell if necessary to pay for food. She decided to offer it to the gatekeeper, if he would let her into the palace. Being a greedy man, he agreed to accept it. He asked for the jewel first, but she refused to pay until she was actually in the room next to the throne. Then she put the jewel into his greedy paw. When the man lifted the curtain, she found herself facing the Emperor who was alone and lying on a couch.

Bowing low, Ti Tuan fell upon her face. The Emperor looked at her kindly and motioned her to rise.

"Who are you and why have you come in this way?" he asked her.

"I am called Ti Tuan, your majesty," she replied, "I beg your pardon for coming in this way, but there was no other way to reach you. I have heard of your great goodness and your justice to all people. I beseech you to give me audience, for I have traveled many miles and have waited long at your door. Only today I paid a great price to see you."

She told the Emperor how she had given her last and most precious possession to the greedy guard to gain admittance. He was angry at this and vowed to punish the guard.

"But now tell me why you wanted so much to see me," he said.

Ti Tuan brought from the folds of her robe the scroll she had written, and read it aloud to him. He listened with amazement to the excellent wording and reasoning. After she had finished reading the description of her father's virtues and innocence and his faithful service, the Emperor asked to examine the scroll and the beautiful handwriting.

"But why do you, a woman, undertake this difficult mission?" he asked at last.

"My father is unfortunate in having no son to defend him," she explained.

The Emperor smiled.

"I am not so sure that he is unfortunate!" he replied. "His daughter seems fully able to undertake the task!"

Ti Tuan bowed.

"Oh, Great One," she said. "I do entreat you for my father that you will pardon him. If you will send to his province and ask the poor peasants there, you will surely find the truth and judge my father innocent."

The Emperor was greatly touched and persuaded by the reasonableness of what she said. He made up his mind to free Schwen and also to pay more attention to the poor of his country.

"Is there anything further that you wish to say?" he asked her.

Ti Tuan nodded.

"Yes, Great One, there is another favor. I do ask that not only my father but all others be saved from the horrible punishments meted out to those who offend the law. For if a person's nose is cut off, or if one's forehead is branded, of what further use is that person to the world and human kind?"

The Emperor was much struck with Ti Tuan's logic about the punishment of prisoners. He also saw how right it was to consider the needs and wishes of the poor, as well as the rich. He decided not only to free Schwen, but he issued an edict that no person was ever to suffer mutilation as a punishment, no matter what the offense had been.

Ti Tuan survives in legend and history as a heroic daughter and a wise and sensible woman.

(From *Tales of A Chinese Amah,* by Ruby F. Kingcome. With permission of James Nisbet & Co., Ltd., Publishers, 22 Berners St., London, WI, 1952.)

Stories About Natural Power and Energy

27
ZOROASTER AND THE SUN

(From Ancient Persia)

Why does the sun seem important enough to be called a "god"?

Z OROASTER WAS A PERSIAN who lived about twenty-five hundred years ago. As a result of deep personal experience, it is said he discovered a whole new way of looking at life. After he had thought through his new ideas, Zoroaster told them to others. He became one of the world's great leaders of religion. A new religion called *Zoroastrianism* was started. Many thousands of people followed his teachings. In Iran and India and other countries of Asia, there are still many who call themselves Zoroastrians. Here is the story about that first great experience.

Zoroaster as a boy had no easy life. In those long-ago days, people did not know much about farming or the raising of sheep and cattle. When rains failed to fall, food became very scarce. Zoroaster knew how it felt to starve. He was often called upon to help the sick.

Being a bright young man, Zoroaster had the best chance his father could give him to learn all that the people of his tribe could teach. He became a pupil of one of the wisest men of his day—one of the magi—who taught him about farming and about taking care of the sick and about the stars and about magic.

But Zoroaster was not satisfied with all these teachings. He kept wanting to know more. He felt very strongly that there was too much trouble and sorrow and sickness and fighting in the world. Why was it that there was so much bad, where there was also so much good?

One day, Zoroaster said to his wife, "I must go away somewhere and be alone. I must have time to think. I feel I must understand what life means and what it is all about."

So he went off alone away from the village—off into the woods and mountains and the lonely desert. There he found a place to sleep in a cave half way up the side of a cliff. He lived for days on wild berries and nuts.

One morning, while the shadows still hung over the sky, he walked out of his cave and down into the long valley below. He walked until he came to the bank of a river. There he plunged himself into the flowing waters and felt refreshed and clean. He felt his mind made clear too. His thoughts were ready once again to struggle with the problem of understanding life.

As he stepped out of the waters onto the bank of the river, he looked up and out over a great plain, toward the east. There before him on the far horizon was the rosy light of the rising sun.

Zoroaster stood motionless, watching as the beams of light slowly lengthened themselves over the sky, reddening into a deeper rose as they spread. He forgot himself. He forgot he was a human being. He could not even see his own shadow because of the brightness around him. He felt as if he were being lifted up from the earth. It seemed to him that a shining angel stood there before him—nine times higher than himself. He thought the angel spoke to him.

"Would you like to come with me to the land of the unseen spirits?" the angel asked. Presently, Zoroaster felt himself going up and up into heaven. There he stood among many

Zoroaster stood motionless, watching as the beams of light slowly lengthened themselves over the sky.

other shining angels and the greatest of all the spirits was there—the great God of Light.

Then one of the angels spoke to him and said, "What is it that you most wish for?" Zoroaster answered, "Above all other things, I wish for goodness."

The angel said, "You have answered well. A good thought is good. A good word is better and a good deed is the best of all."

How long this vision lasted Zoroaster could never tell. The experience was so different from anything he had ever known before that he could not think of the passing of time.

When the spell was over and he began to feel like himself once more, Zoroaster sat down to think. What could it all mean?

His thoughts wandered back to the glorious sunrise he had seen. He said to himself, "How wonderful! The sun rises and it is light. Then the sun sets and it is dark. This happens over and over again regularly. Light and darkness, light and darkness. Over and over!

"Ah! I believe I have it! This universe has in it two great forces—light and darkness. One is good. One is not good. These two forces are continually warring against each other. But the light keeps winning out. So it goes, as long as the world will last.

"There must be two great gods in the universe. The one—the god of light and goodness—we will call Ahura Mazda. The other must be the god of darkness and evil. We will call this god Angri Manyu. This is what life means—a continuous struggle between light and dark, good and evil. This is why there is so much wrong!"

As for himself, Zoroaster decided he would struggle on the side of the God of Light and Goodness—Ahura Mazda—because the sunrise, morning after morning, assured him that in the end goodness would conquer.

It is said that for forty days and forty nights Zoroaster continued to live alone in the wilderness. He had other strange experiences and each time after the spell was gone, he would think over what he had seen.

Finally, by the time he went back to his home and his village, he had much he wanted to tell his people.

Even now, after twenty-five hundred years, Zoroaster's name is honored by thousands of people. To them, any form of light or fire is sacred, for Mazda is the God of Light. Now, although most of us do not think today just as Zoroaster thought long ago, yet the beautiful colors of the sunrise still seem good to us. Since the sun never fails us, but keeps on rising day after day, always and always it reminds us of a God-like power. Its beams of light seem like everlasting arms that bring us a good feeling of support for the goodness in us.

(This story was based on a number of publications, among them, *Zoroaster, the Prophet of Ancient Iran,* by A. V. Williams Jackson; New York: Columbia University Press, 1898-1928; *Zoroaster, the Great Teacher,* by Bernard H. Springett; London: William Rider & Son, 1923; and *The Saviors of Mankind,* by William Van Buskirk; New York: Macmillan, 1929, pp. 112-151.)

28

HOW PROMETHEUS BROUGHT FIRE TO THE WORLD
(From Greece)

How did people get control of fire?

B EFORE THERE WERE ANY ANIMALS or people on earth, according to old Greek legends, great Titans, or Giants inhabited the world. The gods asked one of these giants, called Prometheus, to make some animals for the world. This he did, using earth stuck together with sea water. From the seeds mixed in with the earth and water, these shapes became alive.

To each animal Prometheus gave what it would need to keep alive. To the birds, he gave beaks and wings; to the fish he gave scales and fins. To some animals he gave fur; to others hard shells or tough hide. He made some animals swift to move about and others so that they could hide from enemies. Some received sharp eyes, others keen scent or hearing.

Then Prometheus thought to make something superior to the animals and he kneaded some mud into the form of the gods themselves. But then he had given so much to the other animals that he had hardly anything for his favorite, man. So this first man could not run as fast as the rabbit, nor could he fly like an insect or a bird. He had no fur or feathers or scales to protect his thin skin. His nails were not strong like those of the lion or bear. And he could not see as far as the eagle or smell as did the dog or the deer.

But Prometheus did give man a clever hand and a speaking voice and a superior brain. And Athene, the goddess of wisdom, who admired what Prometheus had done, promised to breathe the spirit of life into the first man.

Yet Prometheus was not satisfied. He flew up into the sky, and as Apollo was passing by in his chariot he caught some fire from the sun with a bundle of reeds. This he brought down to earth and gave to man, showing him how to use it.

For stealing the heavenly fire...Prometheus drew the anger of the gods...

"With fire," Prometheus said, "you can make up for what all the other animals have. Even if your teeth are weak, you can cook your food and be able to eat it. Even if your nails are weak, you can make spears and knives from metal and overcome any animal. Your skin is thin and bare, but fire will help you to use the fur of other animals and make shelters and keep warm wherever you may roam. You will be able to make tools and force the earth to yield more food."

By giving man fire, Prometheus started him off to get ahead of all the other animals, and of many evil spirits too. With fire, man learned to do all kinds of things and to make everything he might want.

However, for stealing the heavenly fire and giving it to man, Prometheus drew the anger of the gods upon himself. They feared that with fire man might become too powerful or too much like themselves. Zeus was especially displeased and resolved to punish Prometheus severely. He had Prometheus chained to the rocky top of high Mount Caucasus. There he suffered the heat of the sun all day and the freezing cold all night. In addition Zeus sent a vulture to tear the body of Prometheus. This went on for a very long time, until Prometheus was finally released by Hercules.

(From *Favorite Stories Old and New* by Sidonie Gruenberg. Published by Doubleday & Co., 1955, pp. 413-414.) Reprint permission granted by the Estate of Sidonie Gruenberg.

29
THE MAIZE SPIRIT

(From the Chippewas of North America)

What do people have to do to get food?

O NCE UPON A TIME, there was a boy, about fourteen, who lived with his family in a small lodge located in a beautiful forest. The boy's father was a hunter who had a great deal of courage and skill, but even so there were times when the family had to go hungry. Of course, one problem was that the boys in the family were not old enough to be of much help.

This boy was cheerful and contented, but he wanted to be helpful to his people. Although it was past time for him to observe the fast for Indian boys of that age, his mother made him a little fasting-lodge so that he could stay alone for his ordeal.

When the lodge was ready for him, he went there and began to meditate upon the goodness of the Great Spirit, who had made all things beautiful in the fields and forests for people to enjoy. The boy deeply longed to help his fellow men. He prayed that he might learn through a dream or in some other way some means for serving.

On the third day of the fast, he was too weak to walk about in the forest. He lay on the ground in his lodge, in a state between sleeping and walking. While he was lying there, a handsome young man came toward him, dressed all in green and wearing beautiful green plumes on his head. The boy liked him at once, but wondered if the young man were only a dream.

"The Great Spirit has heard your prayers," said the hand-some young man. His voice sounded like the wind sighing through the grass. "Do what I tell you and you will have your wish. You will help your people."

"I will do anything you say," the boy declared.

"Wrestle with me, then," said the young man. "Stand up and wrestle with me."

"Wrestle with you?" the boy asked. "But I want you to be my friend."

"I *am* your friend," the young man said. "But you must wrestle with me!"

The boy obeyed then. Although he could hardly stand up because of his weakness, he could still think with his mind and he knew that he must obey. For a long time they struggled silently. When the boy was just about to fall, the young man said, "That will do for today. Tomorrow I shall come again."

On the next day he came again. The boy felt weak and tired. But, strangely enough, the moment he touched the young man, he seemed to have new strength and fought more bravely. At last the young man was forced to cry out that he had had enough.

"You have fought well," he said to the boy. "Tomorrow your trials will end. Your father will be here early to bring you food. In the evening I shall come and wrestle with you again, and this time you will conquer me. I know this because you are destined to win. When you have thrown me, strip off my garments and plumes, bury me where I fall, and then smooth over the earth above me. From that time keep the place moist and clean. Once a month be sure to cover me with fresh earth. And, finally, if you do all this you will one day see me again, clothed in my green robes and wearing my plumes."

When the young man had said this, he vanished. The boy

was sad, for he had learned to care for his wrestling opponent. But he knew that the friend must be obeyed.

The next day, sure enough, his father came with food, but
he decided not to eat immediately. After his father had gone,
the boy sat quietly waiting for his friend to come.

In the evening the young man appeared as he had promised. Although the boy had eaten nothing all day, he seemed
to feel his own strength increasing as he struggled with his
friend. At last he conquered and threw his opponent to the
ground. Sadly then he stripped off the green garments and
plumes and buried the young man in the earth. There was
sorrow in his heart, but he knew that he must obey.

"It is my friend," murmured the boy, *"the friend of my dreams."*

With this task done, he returned to his family and lived with them as he had before. But he did not forget the grave of his friend. Not a weed was allowed to grow on it and once a month he put fresh earth there. He kept it moist and clean. At last he was rewarded. The green plumes rose from the earth and broadened into leaves. When autumn came, a plant stood tall and beautiful and the boy invited his father to come with him to the place. They both looked with wonder at the tall plant, with its waving leaves and golden tassels.

"It is my friend," murmured the boy, "the friend of my dreams."

"It is Mondamin," said his father in wonder. "It is the Spirit of Grain, the gift of the Great Spirit."

And this is the way in which maize was given to the Indians.

(The story has been adapted from *Myths and Legends: The North* Nickerson & Co., Boston, 1914.) Reprint permission granted by Multimedia Publishing Corporation.

Stories About Human
and Spiritual Power

30

GLOOSKAP AND THE BABY

(From the Algonquins of North America)

What are the limits of human power?

G LOOSKAP WAS A GREAT HERO of the Algonquin Indians. According to their stories, he conquered the whole race of giants and magicians and sorcerers, all enemies of mankind, as well as hosts of fiends, goblins, cannibals, and witches. He did it all alone.

But then perhaps fame and good fortune went to his head. Anyway, Glooskap began to brag of his exploits. "I must be the strongest in all the world!" he said many times. Indeed, his friends had to agree with him. So far as they could tell, he was truly the strongest in world. On the other hand, they began to be a little tired of hearing him say so.

One day, he boasted about his greatness to a certain young woman. "It is a pity," he said, "but the truth is there is nothing and no one left for me to subdue!"

To his amazement, the woman laughed. "Are you quite sure of that, Master?" she asked him. "I know of *one* person who remains unconquered."

Glooskap was shocked. "Who is that?" he demanded. "What is his name?"

"He is called Wasis," replied the woman. "But I strongly advise you to have no dealings with *him*!"

Glooskap grunted. He knew that Wasis was only the baby who sat on the floor sucking a piece of maple sugar and

153

crooning a little song to himself.

Now Glooskap had never been married and was quite ignorant about children; so with perfect confidence he smiled at the baby Wasis and asked it to come to him.

The baby smiled at him but did not move.

Glooskap imitated the beautiful song of a certain bird. Wasis paid no heed to him but simply went on sucking his maple sugar.

Glooskap, of course, was not accustomed to being ignored in this way and it made him angry. When he spoke again he shouted and threatened. "Come here to me at once!" he commanded the baby.

Wasis then broke into a howl which quite drowned out Glooskap's loud tones, but he did not move an inch.

Glooskap, now enraged, began reciting magic spells and incantations. He sang the songs that raise the dead. But Wasis seemed to think it was some kind of game and he was getting tired of it and bored. He did not move.

Glooskap, now enraged, began reciting magic spells.

At last Glooskap rushed from the hut in despair. Wasis stayed in his place on the floor. "Goo-goo!" he cried. Then he crowed.

Even now the Indians say that when a baby says "Goo-goo" he is recalling the time when little Wasis conquered the mighty Glooskap.

(This story is taken from *Myths and Legends of the North American Indians,* by Lewis Spence, published by David D. Nickerson & Co., Boston, pp. 145-46, 1914.)

31

THE HUNGRY MULTITUDE

(From the Early Christians)

How can a little food feed many?

T HE STORY WHICH FOLLOWS, nearly two thousand years old, is one of many "miracle" stories about Jesus of Nazareth. It has been told, somewhat differently, by all four of the writers of the Gospels of the New Testament, and has been retold by many later writers. All agree that a marvelous thing happened to a large number of people at that time, through the wisdom and power of the man, Jesus. It is suggested that readers compare this telling of the story with the versions of the Gospels in the New English Translation.

Jesus had just had news of the cruel death of his beloved friend, John the Baptist, and was very sad. He and his disciples had decided to try to escape from the crowds of people who always followed Jesus, so they took a boat across the Sea of Galilee to a lonely place.

But the people heard of this and followed by land, in crowds. When Jesus came ashore and saw the crowds of people already there waiting for him, his heart was so touched that he went out to meet them. Many were sick in heart and body. He talked to them with love and understanding. Many were healed and comforted.

But finally, it became late and the disciples were concerned. They knew that a good many of those people had come without bringing any food along with them and would be hungry.

"We're far from a town here," they said to Jesus. "Hadn't we better send all these folks off to the farms to buy something to eat?"

"But why do you want to send them away?" Jesus asked. "Why don't you give them something to eat yourselves?"

"Well—" Peter said hesitantly, "we could send to the nearest town, I suppose, and buy some food."

"But that would take twenty pounds!" Philip exclaimed. "We don't have that much money!"

"Twenty pounds?" Jesus asked, and smiled. "Well, where shall we get it?"

The boy, the disciples, and the people themselves were amazed.

It was a test question, though, because Jesus knew exactly what he intended to do!

At that moment, Peter's brother, Andrew, came up to them.

"There is a boy here who has five barley loaves and five fishes," he said. "Not much for five thousand people!"

"Bring the boy here," Jesus said, and Andrew brought the boy with his lunch basket. (Andrew was a little embarrassed because he had spoken so hastily.)

"Will you share your lunch with us, little brother?" Jesus asked the boy.

"Oh, yes, sir," the boy replied. "But what can you do with only five loaves and five fishes? They won't go very far."

"They are enough," Jesus replied. He took the loaves and blessed them. Then he took the fishes and blessed them too.

"Thank you, God," he said, "for feeding this multitude."

The crowd had grown silent now. The people began to look at each other with curiosity and wonder.

"Pass the food to the people," Jesus said to his disciples.

Somehow, in a short time, every one was eating! There was enough and some to spare. In fact, when the disciples began to gather up the left-overs, there were several baskets-ful!

The boy, the disciples, and the people themselves were amazed. They simply could not believe what had happened!

"That was a miracle, Master!" Peter cried. "How did it happen? How could you turn so little into so much?"

"There is always enough," Jesus told them. "I did nothing myself. God made it happen!"

(From *The New Testament*, Matthew 14:13-21; Mark 6:30-45; Luke 9:10-17; John 6:1-14. Cf. also Sophia Lyon Fahs, *Jesus, The Carpenter's Son*; Boston: Beacon Press, 1943.)

32

JESUS AND THE EVIL SPIRITS

(From the Early Christians)

How can a person's spirit be healed?

J ESUS AND THE THREE DISCIPLES , Peter, James, and John, had had an overwhelming and exhausting week up in the mountains. Some wonderful things had happened to them there. On the way down, however, Jesus suggested that they not discuss the experience with other people.

"They wouldn't understand," he said. "They are not ready yet. You must be patient."

But when they came to the place where the rest of the disciples were waiting, they found the usual large crowd milling about and, as usual, arguing about Jesus.

"There are some lawyers among them," Peter observed. "They seem determined to give Jesus trouble, I'm afraid."

"And the rest of us, too," observed Peter.

But when the people saw Jesus, they were overcome with awe, even the lawyers, and ran forward to greet him.

"What are you all arguing about?" he asked them. (Jesus was tired and a little out of patience.)

One of the men in the crowd spoke up.

"Master," he said, "I don't know what the rest of these people were arguing about, but I came to bring my son to see if you can help him."

"What is the trouble?" Jesus asked.

"It is a spirit that seems to possess him," the man said. "He

159

can't walk. And whenever the spirit attacks him, it knocks him to the ground and he foams at the mouth and grinds his teeth and goes all stiff. It's terrible. He is a good lad, too, when the spirit leaves him alone."

"But why did you wait for me?" Jesus asked. "Why didn't you do something yourself?"

"Oh, I did!" the man assured him. "I asked your disciples to get rid of the spirit, but they couldn't do it."

Jesus was really exasperated then.

"What unbelievers you people are!" he exclaimed. "What are you going to do when I'm gone? I can't be here forever to take care of you. I wonder just how long I'll have to put up with you!"

It wasn't like Jesus to talk like that! Peter and James looked at each other in astonishment.

"It just isn't like the Master!" Peter whispered.

Jesus looked sorry then and said to the man, "Bring the boy to me."

The father brought the boy forward at once and immediately the evil spirit seemed to seize him. He fell on the ground and rolled over and over, foaming at his mouth.

Jesus shook his head. "How long has he been like this?" he asked.

"Ever since he was a baby," his father said. "Sometimes the spirit has even tried to kill my son by throwing him into the fire or into the river. O Jesus, if it is possible, please take pity on us and help us!"

"If it is *possible,* did you say?" Jesus exclaimed. "Good heavens, man, *all* things are possible if one has faith!"

"I have faith, Sir!" the man cried. "But help me where my faith falls short!"

Jesus saw then that the crowd, now quieter, was pressing about and he acted quickly before they could come too close.

"Deaf and dumb spirit," he said, "I command you, come out of this boy and never bother him again!"

The spirit screamed and shrieked (through the mouth of the boy) and racked the boy's body fiercely. Finally, the boy fell down and then was quiet. But he was very white and some of the people thought that he was dead. A murmuring began.

The boy raised his head, and then stood up. It was a great moment. The crowd was abashed and shrank away. The boy and his father went with them. And at last Jesus and his disciples were alone.

The crowd was abashed and shrank away.

The disciples were silent until finally Andrew spoke.

"Why couldn't we do it, Master?" he asked. "We tried — we tried! Why couldn't we drive out the spirit?"

Jesus understood. "You can," he said. "But there must be prayer and faith. It was necessary for all of you — that man and his son, and yourselves—to *believe* you could do it. Where there is faith, all things are possible."

(From *The New Testament,* Matthew 17:14-21; Mark 9:14-29.)

33

THE BOY WHO ASKED QUESTIONS

(From England)

How can a human being discover the secrets of the universe?

ISAAC NEWTON WAS BORN NEARLY 400 years ago on a farm in the small village of Woolsthorpe, England. His father died before he was born, so Isaac and his mother lived alone on the family farm during his childhood. He did rather poorly in school. When he finally finished all the grades in his village school, his mother decided he should stay home and work on the farm, as his father had done.

Fortunately, she discovered a little later that the trouble with Isaac was not that he was dull, but that he didn't find books as interesting as all the natural things in the outdoors about him. And, although he wasn't fond of pulling weeds from the garden, he was always curious about the wild animals in the woods.

One time, Isaac invented a toy windmill which operated without wind. (A mouse was substituted!) He made kites of different shapes and sizes. One afternoon, instead of working on his spelling lesson, he worked out a way to measure the speed of the wind. In fact, he did so many interesting things as a boy and cared so little about farming that his mother finally decided to send him to the university after all. He went to Cambridge University where the professors recognized his unusual intelligence. Before Isaac graduated, they said that he was better with numbers than anyone else at the university.

His time at study was interrupted by an epidemic of the black plague which brought death to many thousands at that time. So critical was the epidemic that the university had to close for two years. Isaac spent the time back home on the farm, of course. Perhaps it was a good thing too because, except for that time on the farm, the famous *apple* episode might never have happened!

The story is told of a day when Isaac Newton saw an apple fall from a tree in the orchard. It made him curious. He remembered how Galileo had dropped balls of different sizes and weights from the Leaning Tower of Pisa in order to find how fast each fell to the ground. Isaac remembered that Galileo thought the balls kept increasing their speed as they fell closer to the ground because of a power—a pulling power of the earth which Galileo called "gravity."

Isaac Newton asked himself other questions. He saw the moon shining above and wondered how it could stay up there. What kept it from falling to the earth like the apple? What kept the moon going round and round the earth?

Now, if Isaac Newton had asked the neighbors in the village those questions, they probably would have said to him, "God put the moon up in the sky. God told the moon to go round and round the earth and the moon is obeying God. Or perhaps an angel is pulling the moon around."

But Isaac was not satisfied with answers like these. He thought that some much greater plan must be in process. As he wondered and thought, he made a great big guess.

Perhaps, he thought, this pull of the earth that Galileo called "gravity" reaches all the way to the moon. Perhaps it has something to do with why the moon keeps circling this way, almost as if some force were trying to bring it all the way down, but was not quite strong enough to do that! Perhaps the moon is so far away that the pull of gravity is not strong enough to make it tumble down out of the sky. Or perhaps some other opposing force is pushing it outward from the circling path around the earth, but gravity is just strong enough to keep the moon moving at a certain speed in a regular path around and around the earth.

Or perhaps some other opposing force is pushing it outward from the circling path around the earth.

Isaac thought about how large the earth is. Scientists in his time had determined that it was about 21,000 miles in circumference and they thought that the moon was about 250,000 miles away. So Isaac Newton began to work out a long and hard arithmetic problem. His problem was to find out just how much pull the earth would have on the moon and how this would affect the movement of the moon each day for a whole month. According to the way his figures came out, the moon ought to go around the earth in thirty-two days.

But everyone knew, and Newton himself knew, that the moon takes only *twenty-eight* days to go around the earth. He was very much disappointed. Something was wrong, but he did not know just what the mistake could be. Finally, he put his papers away in a drawer and began to be curious about other things.

Years went by. Isaac went back to the university to study and became a professor. In fact, sixteen years passed before he worked again on that arithmetic problem about the moon. Then one day a visitor from France reported to him that a scientist in Paris had discovered the old measurement of the earth to be wrong! Instead of being 21,000 miles around at the equator, it was 25,000 miles around. This meant that the earth had more pull on the moon than his earlier figures had shown.

Newton rushed to his room, forgot to eat dinner, and began to work again on the long arithmetic problem he had done sixteen years before. It is said he became so excited that he couldn't figure straight! This man who was famous for being the greatest mathematician in the university was so keyed up that he couldn't add or divide without making mistakes! Finally, he sent the problem to a friend and said, "I'm too nervous. Please finish it for me!" After some days, the answer came that he was waiting and hoping for. According to the law of gravity and these new figures, the moon ought to take only twenty-eight days to go around the earth! And it does just that! Newton had *proved* that the earth's gravitation controls the speed of the moon around the earth.

It was one of the great moments in history. Finding the

answer to this one question seemed to open the door to many more questions: Why does the earth move around the sun? Why do other planets go on their rounds? Do all the heavenly bodies have gravity? Is there one rule or law by which all the stars and all the planets move? Do all things everywhere happen according to some planned orderliness?

If all this is so, how different the world and everything everywhere must be from what people had so long supposed! No longer could it be true that an angel kept the moon from falling and pulled it around the earth, as men had so often said. It was *gravity,* and gravity could be measured! But is gravity in the sun also? And does the sun's gravity keep our earth whirling around it? Why don't the stars all fall down on us? Is there gravity in everything, pulling things together, but with other counterbalancing pulls (such as centrifugal force) keeping them from smashing into one another?

Isaac Newton's picture of the universe was startling. It was puzzling too. Where was God, then? Weren't there angels any more? Each question seemed to lead on to another question and gave a new clue for answering it.

The book which Newton wrote describing his findings is called *Principia.* It has been regarded by some as one of the ten greatest books ever written, since it gave mankind a new key by which to open new doors to more understanding of the universe.

Before Newton died, he was highly honored. Today, after more than three hundred years, the stories of his discoveries are still retold throughout the world. We call him one of mankind's greatest scientists and one of the world's great men. But Newton thought of himself very humbly! He felt that what he had learned was only a very small beginning of what there was still to learn.

When he was an old man and his friends were talking about him one day, he said this: "I know not what people may think about what I have discovered. For myself, I feel that I have been like a child playing on the seashore, now and then finding some prettier pebble or more beautiful shell than my companions, while the unbounded ocean of truth lies undiscovered before me.''

(Condensed from *Worshipping Together with Questioning Minds,* by Sophia Lyon Fahs, Published by the Beacon Press, Boston, 1965, pp. 82-88. Used by permission of Unitarian Universalist Association.)

34

THE POLLUTION DRAGON

(A modern fable created by children)

Why can people do together
what one person cannot do alone?

A LONG TIME AGO, THERE LIVED a mean pollution dragon. He was black and huge, with big spikes down his back. He lived in a big, very, very dirty smelly dump. One day people had thrown all their trash in this place and the trash had made the shape of a mean dragon, and the dragon had come to life.

The dragon ate trees and flowers and, worst of all, he couldn't seem to fill his stomach fast enough. When he had eaten all the trees and flowers, he began to eat the trash in the dump. This trash made him big and clumsy and, while he was digesting it, the fire in his stomach (he was a fiery dragon) made horrible, dreadful, awful, ghastly, yucky, black smoke which quickly covered the earth.

Also, because the dragon was so clumsy, he bumped into things and stepped on people and scattered garbage and trash around to make a dirtier earth. He liked to swim in Lake Ontario (next to the dump, it was his favorite place) and he would splash around, having fun. He loved the phosphates because they were one of his favorite foods. He messed up the lake with his splashing and, because his body was so dirty, he made the water dirty too.

169

He liked to swim in Lake Ontario.

People got worried about the dragon and wondered how to get rid of him. They were mad at him for eating all the trees and flowers. They didn't mind his eating trash; in fact, they thought it was a good way to get rid of it, but they couldn't stand the mess he made and they were having trouble breathing the awful smoke. The dragon was so big and mean that nobody dared to go out and fight him, and they couldn't figure out a way to kill him. Some people actually seemed to want to breathe the smoke and live with the mess and do without trees and flowers rather than spend their time thinking up a plan.

A child finally had a great idea. The child suggested that if all the people would stop making so much trash (in fact, any trash at all) they could starve the dragon and he would die. The idea was so simple that nobody had thought of it, but news of it spread quickly.

After a while, nobody took trash to the dump any more. They found ways of using the trash they made and they thought up ways to make practically no trash at all.

This took a lot of effort and time, but soon the dragon got weaker and didn't even leave the dump to go for his swim in the lake. Trees and flowers began to come back and the people realized how much they had missed them. As the dragon became still weaker, the smoke began to clear up and soon the people could breathe easily again.

When the people hadn't seen or heard the dragon for a few days, a group of them went to the dump to see what was happening. They didn't see a dragon, but they found a pile of trash in a familiar shape and they knew that he wouldn't bother them any more. They had killed the mean pollution dragon themselves. They were very happy and they promised never to let such an awful thing happen again.

(Composed by children in Grades 1-3 at the First Unitarian Church School, Rochester, New York, Spring, 1971.) Reprint permission granted by Elizabeth Strong Taylor, Religious Education Director. First Unitarian Church, Rochester, N.Y.

Stories About the Meaning of Living and Dying

35

MAWU'S WAYS
ARE BEST

*(from Benin, formerly Dahomey,
in Africa)*

Why does everybody have to die?

PERHAPS THE BELIEF ABOUT GOD described in "Mawu's
Ways are Best" may be hard to understand and to accept
today. However, we need to accept this idea only as the way
some people in ancient times felt about God. Not all people,
even in those days, thought or believed in the same way. But
when the Dahomeys tried to find a reason for some of the
strange and terrible things which they saw happening all
around them, they decided that "Mawu's Way" offered the
only explanation which seemed to make sense to them. See
what you feel about it.

In ancient times, Mawu sent a messenger to earth every
day to travel from sunrise to sunset. He did this all the time,
every year.

One day, while on his errands the messenger reached a
place called Admala. When he arrived in Admala, it was
already night. He could go no more, so he went to a house.
There was a man on the road also and, as night fell, the man
too went into this house. The people gave them places in the
same room—the two strangers together.

Mawu's messenger asked the man where he was going and

the man said, "I am going to where the sun sets."

"Good," said Mawu's messenger. "It is life that gives a companion! I myself am going to where the sun sets. Let us go together."

The next morning, at first cock crow, in a house near the one where they were sleeping, they heard crying. The parents were crying because their child was sick. Mawu's messenger went to that house and asked the parents why they cried. "Why haven't you slept all night?" he asked.

"We have a child here who is very sick," they said.

"Very well," said Mawu's messenger. He took a sack from his possessions and out of it some powder. He gave some of that powder to the father of the sick child. Then he went back quickly to the man who would be traveling with him and said to him, "Wake up! Wake up! We must go at once."

They had taken only a few steps away from the village when all at once the people in the house of the sick child began to shout. "Where is the stranger?" they cried. "Where is the stranger?" The child was dead.

But the messenger and his companion were already far from there. They went until they came to a place called Savalou and there they spent the night, taking shelter in a house beside the road.

At first cock crow, Mawu's messenger took some flint and made a fire. Then he put the fire to the straw of the house where they had slept. Having done this, he said to the man, his companion, "Wake up, wake up! We must be going!"

After they left, the whole house began to burn.

The people in nearby houses asked, "Where are the strangers who slept here? Where are they?"

But they were already far away. The messenger and his companion ran and continued their journey.

The man, who was a human being, was astonished by all this.

He did not know that the other was a messenger of Mawu.

He had never seen anyone behave as this one did. But he said nothing as yet and they came near to a place called Badahwedgi where the sun sets.

Now there was a river that separated Badahwedgi from where the two travelers were. In order to cross the river, it was necessary to put down a raft and pass over on it. There was an old man from Badahwedgi who was in the habit of coming to the river bank for leaves. He gathered them and then went back. Now he was crossing the river for a second time. So Mawu's messenger followed the old man who was going slowly and cautiously. Mawu's messenger came behind the man and pushed him so that he fell into the water.

When he did this, the other traveler was frightened and began to run away, but Mawu's messenger called him back. "Come, come here," he said. "You are going the wrong way. We are almost to the place where the sun sets."

The other one stopped, but did not come back. "What I saw on the river here is too much," he said. "I must run away from it."

Mawu's messenger explained then. "I am not a man," he said. "I know you are astonished at all I did. But I did it because I knew it must be. It was Mawu's will that the child should die in that house back there. If I had not given it the powder, both its mother and father would have died when it took its first step. It was Mawu who sent me to destroy that child."

"But what about the house which you burned?" the man asked.

"Mawu sent me to burn the house," the messenger said. "The family had rich relatives among them who had buried all their money under that house. The people living there did not know it and they were poor. Now, when they begin to dig in the earth to build a new house, they will find the money."

"And the man who fell into the river?" the traveler asked.

"That was Mawu's will also," the messenger said. "I made

We are almost to the place where the sun sets.

the man fall into the river because the king of Badahwedgi is dead and a new king must be named. If that old man were alive, they could not name a young one king. But it is right that there should be a young king. If that old man were king there would be no more goats, no more cattle, no more children in the kingdom. With a young king, they will have goats, pigs, and children also."

Then he said, "I look into the hearts of men because Mawu has sent me to look. You must not be astonished. This is Mawu's way of getting things done. There must always be death so that there can be life. Year after year I do this service for Mawu and when, in the course of life, you see these things happening you will know that it is Mawu who wills them, and Mawu is just. Men cannot see all, as Mawu sees. Mawu's ways are always best."

(From *Dahomean Narrative: A Cross-cultural Analysis* by Melville J. and Frances S. Herskovits, Evanston: Northwestern University Press, 1958, pp. 152-54. Reprinted with permission of the Northwestern University Press.)

36
THE SOLDIER DREAMS

(From the Buddhists)

When you die, is that the end of you?

A SOLDIER OF INDIA AND A WISE MAN, named Kessapa, were talking together. The soldier had just said he did not think that any one could live after dying because, when a person was dying, no one had ever seen a soul come out of the body.

"So," said the soldier, "there cannot be any soul."

But the wise man answered the soldier in this way:

"Soldier, do you remember how the other afternoon you were taking a nap in your house and while you were sleeping you dreamed that you were walking about in a beautiful grove? Do you remember how, in your dream, you delighted in walking through the cool woods and across the open field? Do you remember how, in your dream, you sat down beside a lovely pond all filled with the large white blossoms of the lotus flower?"

"Yes," said the soldier. "I well remember my delightful dream of the lotus pond and the cool woods."

"Were people watching you while you were having your nap?" the wise man asked the soldier.

"Yes," said the soldier, "there were people about me all the time."

"Did these people see you walking through the woods or

sitting down beside the lotus pond?"

"No, my dear sir, of course they did not see."

"What was it, then, that walked through the woods and sat down beside the lotus pond? Do we not call that your soul?" asked the wise man. "Could these people see your soul when it came out of your body or when it went back into your body?"

"You dreamed that you were walking in a beautiful grove."

"No, they could not see my soul at all," said the soldier.

"Well, then, soldier, if people cannot see what is really, really you, when you are living and dreaming, how can you expect them to see the part of you that we call the 'soul' leave the body when you are dying?"

But the soldier was still wondering. He understood and yet he did not understand.

("The Soldier Dreams" is adapted and retold from the story, "We Cannot See the Soul During Life," pp. 109-116, in *Buddhist Parables,* translated from Pali by E. W. Burlingame. Yale University Press: New Haven, 1922.) Reprint permission granted by Yale University Press.

37

MPOBE,
THE HUNTER
(From Uganda)

Where do people go when they die?

O NCE UPON A TIME, there lived a man called Mpobe. He was a hunter and he had a dog which went hunting with him. Because the jungle is very thick in the Uganda forests, Mpobe tied a bell to his dog for fear it might become lost.

When Mpobe and his dog had been hunting for some time, a little animal that the people called a "musu" ran out of the jungle grass. The dog gave chase, with Mpobe running after them as fast as he could.

On they went through the jungle and it seemed as if the musu would never be caught. At last, however, it ran into a hole and the dog followed it. When Mpobe came up, he found the hole, which looked like the entrance to a tunnel. As he heard the dog's bell tinkling far away, he ran into the hole and followed it. On and on they went in the dark, down into the earth.

Suddenly, the tunnel came to an end. Mpobe found himself in a strange country, right down in the center of the Earth. It was a beautiful country with lovely gardens and trees and flowers and rivers. There were flocks of sheep and goats and herds of cattle grazing in green fields.

But still the musu ran on and the dog ran after it. Mpobe followed them, looking from side to side as he ran and wondering at all he saw. At last they came to a courtyard.

Although the dog had not caught the musu, the two stopped and rested quietly together. A very old man sat alone in the middle of the courtyard.

Mpobe knelt down and greeted the old man who said to him, "What are you doing here and why have you come?"

"Sir," said Mpobe, "I do not know where I am. This is my dog and we were hunting this musu above in the jungle. The musu ran into a hole, my dog followed it, I followed the dog and we arrived here!"

Then the old man said, "Do you know who I am?" Mpobe said he did not.

"I am Walumbe," said the old man. "When I go to the Earth and carry away people and cows and sheep and goats, I bring them all down here to my beautiful country of Death. No one can go back again. You and the musu and your dog must stay forever, now that you are here."

Mpobe cried bitterly and implored Walumbe to allow him to return. "I will not stay long," he said. "I will come back soon. Just let me go and say good-bye to my friends."

Walumbe said, "I will let you go on one condition. You must tell nobody what you have seen or where you have been. If you will promise me to keep this a secret, you may go back. But as sure as you tell it to anyone, I will come for you and then you must return here forever!"

Mpobe promised gladly and the old man showed him the way back. When he got home, his mother and his wife and his relatives rejoiced very much. He had been away for three days and they thought he must have been lost in the jungle. Of course, they asked him where he had been and what he had seen, but to all questions he made the same reply, "I was hunting a musu and I lost my way."

This went on for many days and he would tell them nothing; so they finally got tired of asking. But one day he was alone in the house with his old mother and she asked him again, "Mpobe, my child, tell me what you saw in the jungle."

"I cannot tell you," he said. "I promised I would keep it quite secret."

But his mother insisted. "Who made you promise?" she asked. "Can't you tell your old mother a little about it?"

At last Mpobe said to her, "Will you promise to tell no one if I tell you where I went and what I saw in those three days in the jungle?"

"Whom should I tell, my child?" his mother asked. "Isn't my heart yours?"

On they went in the dark, down into the earth.

Then Mpobe told her all about his hunting and the musu and the tunnel, and the wonderful country in the middle of the Earth, and the very old man who was Walumbe.

That night, when everything was quiet and still, Mpobe heard a voice calling, "Mpobe! Mpobe!"

When he answered, "Here am I!" the voice went on, "I am Walumbe. You have broken your promise. You must come with me, and this time there is no return!" Together they went into the jungle.

In the morning when his friends found that Mpobe was gone, they wondered if he were hunting again, but his old mother told them the story. They all went into the jungle and looked for the tunnel which leads to Walumbe's country.

Although they searched for a long time, and many people have searched for it since then, no one has ever found the tunnel and no one has ever seen Walumbe when he visits the Earth.

("Mpobe, the Hunter" was taken from *The King of the Snakes and Other Folk-lore Stories from Uganda* by Rosetta Gage (Mrs. George) Baskerville, published by Sheldon Press, London, 1922. Permission received from Sheldon Press of London for use in this edition.)

38

THE KING'S QUESTION

(From the Buddhists)

What will we be like after we die?

K ING MILINDA WHO LIVED LONG, LONG AGO in Bactria, in
Afghanistan, was a very thoughtful man and always full
   f u l l
of questions. But there were no libraries in that long-ago
time to which he could go and borrow books to read. Nor
was there any college with professors where he could go to
study. There were, however, here and there a few great
teachers to whom people could go and of whom they could
ask questions. Men would walk long distances or if they had
carriages they would ride, in order to sit down with other
questioners. Day after day in some quiet study spot they
would listen to one of these teachers.

Nagasena was such a teacher, very widely known throughout India. King Milinda had heard about Nagasena and at
last decided to have his charioteer drive him all the way to
the teacher's home where he might stay a while and ask the
wise man some questions. This is a story, said to have been
told by Buddha, about how one morning Nagasena answered
one of King Milinda's questions.

A small group of people from different places was sitting
in a circle on the grassy ground with Nagasena leading the

185

conversation.

"Honorable teacher," said King Milinda, "I very much want to know what you think about our living after dying. If I do live again, for example, will I be the same person I am now? Or will I be a different person?"

"You will not be the same person, nor will you be a different person, my friend," said Nagasena.

You will not be the same person, nor will you be a different person.

The king did not understand.

"Well, let us put it in a different way," the teacher continued. "You are now a man, but once you were a small baby, not even able to sit up or talk. Are you the same person now that you were then?"

King Milinda thought for a moment and then said, "I think I would say that the little baby lying on its back was one person and that I, now, am a different person."

"Well, then," said Nagasena, "how about the mother of that little baby—is she your mother?"

King Milinda was puzzled. He hesitated.

The teacher continued, "Can it be, O King, that the mother of that baby is one person and that the mother of the baby who grew up to be a king is another person? Is your mother another person now?"

"No, that cannot be," said King Milinda. "But how about you, O Nagasena? Suppose you asked this same question of yourself. What would you say?"

"I would say, O great King, that I myself was once a small baby lying on my back and that the same *I* is now a man. Perhaps, if I tell you a story, it will be plainer."

King Milinda nodded and the teacher continued.

"A certain man owned a big garden of mango trees that were full of fruit. One night a thief entered the garden and stole all the mangoes off the trees. He fled, with bushel baskets full of them.

"The owner finally discovered who the thief was. He was arrested and brought before the king to be punished.

"The owner then said to the king: 'Your Majesty, this man is a thief, for he stole all my mangoes. They are my mangoes because they grew in the garden that I planted.'

"Then the thief said, 'Your Majesty, I did not steal this man's mangoes. They were not his mangoes. All that he owned were the seeds he planted. The seeds this man planted were one kind of thing, and the mangoes that I stole are entirely different things. I am not guilty of stealing *his* mangoes.'"

"Now," said the teacher to Milinda, "if you had been the judge, what would you have said? Would the man be guilty or not?"

"Certainly, the man would be a thief," said King Milinda.

"For what reason would he be a thief?" asked Nagasena.

"No matter what the thief might say, noble Sir, he could

not deny that the mangoes he took came from the seeds the man had planted. So, of course, the mangoes that grew from the seeds were his, too. The man who stole them was a thief."

"Precisely so, great King," said Nagasena. "No matter what the man might say, the mangoes he stole came straight from the seeds that the owner had planted. The seeds and the plants and the trees and the fruit on the trees all belong together. They are one and the same, even though they seem so different."

"So it is with us, O King Milinda. We all have come straight from small seeds. These grew in our mothers' bodies. First, we were seeds, then we were babies, then we were children, and now we are men. Yet, we are still the same persons, but how very different from what we were long ago!" He smiled. "The thought gives us much to wonder about, does it not?"

"So I think it will be after we die. We shall be the same persons we are now, yet we shall be so different we will not seem like the same persons at all. Who among us is wise enough to understand? To be a person, living—changing continuously—yet, remaining the same!"

Then King Milinda knew there was no man anywhere who could answer his question, and he wondered—would he ever know?

("The King's Question" is adapted and retold from the stories, "Theft of Mangos," "Seeds and Plants," and "Embryo and Child," pp. 204–207 and p. 211 in *Buddhist Parables,* translated from Pali by E. W. Burlingame. Yale University Press: New Haven, 1922.) Reprint permission granted by Yale University Press.

39

BRAHMAN, THE UNIVERSAL BEING

(From the Hindus)

What does it mean to "live forever"?

MANY CENTURIES AGO, thoughtful men and women of India were trying to express the inexpressible, to explain the inexplainable, to imagine the invisible. They sang this hymn to creation:

> "In the beginning there was nothing
> The bright sky was not; the earth was not,
> Neither was there day nor night;
> Nor life nor death.
> In the beginning only THAT was, THAT which is
>   imperishable,
> THAT which alone is real."

Here is the story, as the Hindus tell it, of how all things began:

In the beginning, on an unknown day that was neither day nor night, the warm first waters were planted with the eternal seed of life. How this could be, who can know? Or how this seed grew into an egg, shining like a star, yet more brilliant than any star—who can say? Or how this first egg burst its

189

shell, and Brahman came forth, who can know? Brahman, the Creator, the Imperishable. One within all that perishes! The Unchanging One in all that changes! *Brahman* was born!

Brahman's days and nights were each a thousand ages long; each age was as long as four million three hundred and twenty thousand mortal years. During these long ages, Brahman multiplied his strength, his mind, his purposes, and he put a part of himself into every new thing he created. Thus Brahman became the all-encompassing, all-containing life in every man, beast, flower, and stone, and in the earth and in the stars.

When he created man, Brahman gave different parts of

And he put a part of himself into every new thing he created.

himself to different people so that there might be many kinds of persons, each able to do something that was needed by the rest. To one group, or caste, who sprang from his mouth and brain, he gave mental ability to study the sacred books and to teach and lead others in rituals and ceremonies. To another group, who sprang from his arms, Brahman gave the power to be warriors and kings. To a third group, who sprang from his thighs, he gave the power to be farmers and cattle-men and traders. To a fourth group, or caste, who sprang from his feet, Brahman gave the duty to be servants, and doers of common tasks.

Thus, to each human being Brahman assigned a special kind of life, and certain duties. This was called one's *dharma*. The king's dharma was different from the slave's *dharma*. A woman's *dharma* was different from a man's. But to each one there was assigned a place, and that person, and his or her children and grandchildren were to continue to follow the special *dharma* given by the Creator, Brahman.

To *all* human beings there was given a common *dharma* or duty. This was to respect all living things, to be truthful, not to steal, to be kind and compassionate, and self-constrained. Most of all, each one must find freedom from the idea of "me" and "mine."

The life which Brahman implanted in every living being, the Hindus said, is imperishable. It is eternal and the eternal is everywhere. In a person, this living essence is called the *atman* (we might call this the "spirit"). Death can never destroy it. When one person dies, the *atman* (or spirit) of that person will eventually be born in another life form. If the person has led a good life, the *atman* will rise to a new level in the life to come. One of a lower caste may be born into a higher one. But if the life lived is not good, the *atman* or spirit will be reborn into a lower caste, or even perhaps in the body of a beast.

Thus, every time the person's body dies, the *atman,* or

spirit, that lives in it, starts anew up the ladder of life (or down, as the case may be). If it keeps on going up with each new body, it will go higher and higher until finally it is worthy to be absorbed again into the life of the All-encompassing One—Brahman, the ocean of all being. This is salvation. This is the highest goal — union with the divine All-in-One. This is Nirvana. When Nirvana is attained, all death and sorrow will have passed away, for this *atman*.

How many births or deaths one has had before the present birth, none may know. But one thing is sure. One's present place in society (the caste, or animal form) is due to the kinds of lives one has lived in earlier incarnations. Every word, thought, and deed brings its own reward or punishment. There is no escape. The way may be long, but progress is sure for the one who tries to do well.

Brahman is forever patient and kind. Brahman never hurries the consequences of one's wrong-doings. No one will ever be cast into hell to suffer forever. Brahman, the Hindus said, expects every person to find the way eventually back to Nirvana. Some choose one way, some another; some will create one image of the unknowable and invisible, some another. "The countless gods are only my million faces," said Brahman. "Whoever comes to me through whatever religion, I reach that person," said Brahman. "All are struggling in the paths that lead ultimately to me."

What did the Hindus imagine this final reunion with Brahman would be like? The Hindu scriptures give some clues through their description of the death of their spiritual hero-savior, Lord Krishna. When Lord Krishna died, they said, his visible body disappeared. Its divine invisible nature diffused its creative life all around, within all that is visible everywhere. The Imperishable became dissolved in the perishable. The Unchanging became immersed in all that changes. The *atman* of Krishna and Brahman again became one.

(Based on extracts from an unpublished manuscript, "India's Story of Krishna," by Sophia Lyon Fahs. Source cited is *The Bhagavad-Gita: The Song of God,* as translated by Swami Probhavenanda and Christopher Isherwood. The latest edition of this old sacred book was published by the Vendanta Society of Southern California, Hollywood, California, in 1972, which has given permission for use of selected items. However, more comprehensive resources on Hindu beliefs were obviously tapped. The initial poem appears to be a simplification for children by the author herself of Hymn 129, "Creation," from the very early Hindu scriptures, the *Rigveda,* of which there are numerous translations.)

A Word to Parents and Teachers

Why a Book of "Old Tales" for Today's Children?

Children are naturally full of curiosity. They are forever asking questions. They want to know why, and who, and when, and how. They wonder who the first person was, how the world got started, and where they themselves came from. They are fiercely concerned about what seems right to them, or what seems wrong. Once they sense a problem, they begin to look for an answer.

In this yearning to know — to understand — of course they are not alone. From the beginning of time, people, old and young, have been asking the same questions about the world around them and about life and its meaning. Every culture has created its own map of things as they seem to be. Some of these answers take the form of myths or legends which are usually simple stories that appeal to children. They are easy to follow and understand, yet often profound in their deeper meaning. By reliving in imagination the experience of people who lived long ago, children today can share in the universal creative process as they struggle for answers to the same universal questions. The book, *Old Tales for a New Day,* was planned to help in that process.

But why are these old stories important for today? Why not use contemporary material for teaching, and why not deal with today's situations? There are certainly plenty to choose from, real to children, and right here on our own doorsteps. Why cloud the issues with strange talk from people who lived ten thousand years ago?

For one thing, there is a certain advantage to pondering questions in a context removed from present-day experience. Such issues are too likely to be weighted for most people, and to have one or another kind of personal investment or bias.

But there is also intrinsic worth in the ancient stories. More and more modern scholars are coming to believe that in the thinking of ancient people we can find important clues for living today; for example, in diet, medicine, music, and the dance. Also, as we have suggested, there seems to be in the old stories a core of thought that touches the fundamental and universal. Often, the ancient teller of tales was struggling for an idea or a feeling that rings true today, even to the modern scholar or philosopher.

The questions dealt with in these stories are independent of time and place. They are questions about life and death, about the mysteries of existence, about the nature of good and evil. Through sharing the search with people of long ago, children can learn to cultivate for themselves a "world view" and world sympathies that will be their own—that will find them strong when they need support, yet open to change when new experience and knowledge require it, and secure to cope with today's welter of confused values and uncertain goals.

The stories in this book are not a random selection. They have been carefully selected from a sampling of thousands of stories. To help children with the growing process, their emphasis is on positive values and on issues of concern today. They were also drawn from a wide variety of cultural perspectives. Their strangeness to modern readers stems in part from the image of the supernatural created when ancient people looked for something outside, and bigger and more powerful than themselves—something that might be responsible for their troubles and their good fortune. Urged on by certain universal impulses — the impulse to save one's life in the presence of danger, the push of curiosity, the desire to be with, and loved by, others — they needed to explain, to supplicate, to make amends, to bargain.

The significance of the stories is not always obvious. This fact can be the stimulus to independent thought and discovery. Even if a "lesson" is spelled out, the readers are sufficiently removed from the source to be able to question and compare.

Children should be encouraged to think of *Old Tales for a New Day* as a book to be enjoyed — a book of unusual, sometimes puzzling stories, which they can read and think about themselves, or listen to and discuss with others.

The central goal of the collection, however, is that it be used, either by parents or group leaders, in teaching. Each story begins with a lead question identifying a core issue, and is intended to stimulate thought and bring out other questions for discussion. Further questions for group use, as well as activities and additional resources are suggested in a separately published study guide, entitled *Exploring Basic Issues With Young People.*

Another learning instrument is provided in Gobin Stair's unusual and thought-provoking illustrations. Many of these "speak in symbols" so that children will have the excitement of interpreting for themselves the special messages of picture and story. The accompanying study guide suggests ways of using each one of the illustrations in teaching.

A guide to pronunciation of words which may be unfamiliar is included at the end of the book.

When *Old Tales* is used in teaching, it is important that some attention be given to the culture from which each story comes, and that the readers recognize and respect the real worth of the thinking represented. For example, "The Fig Tree and the Seed" from India presents a rather sophisticated concept of universal spirit. Oddly enough, this seems to cause no difficulty whatsoever to children. The pervasive quality of spirit, or truth, or power, or whatever it may be called, is more easily understood than explained, and the story carries conviction. Remarkable insights into human character can come out of discussions of this story.

Some stories deal with problems people have always had in getting along with each other—problems related to reward and punishment, conflict, and possessions. Others focus on love and loyalty. Still others attempt to cope with issues related to death and dying.

Grown-ups will find "The Half-Boy of Borneo" interesting because it deals with a great psychological problem lying deep in each one of us. "Half-Boy" is really a parable about the struggle within each person between two parts—the good and the bad, the social and rational and the primitive instinctive urges.

The collection includes three stories dealing with the problem of war, not unfamiliar to early people. "What is Worth Fighting For?" from India asks if the life of a person is not more important than the winning of a battle. The Krishna story deals with questions of whether or not war is *ever* justified.

The question of women's liberation did not begin with the present generation either. Apparently, the ancients were also asking if men were more intelligent than women and whether there is such a thing as "men's work" or "women's work." "The River of Separation" will not satisfy everybody with its conclusion, but teachers and parents may be interested in seeing how their children respond to it!

Special care has been given to those eternal, still unanswered questions about "living and dying." Children cannot escape them. They can and usually do avoid talking about them when talking to adults. But the authors believe that it is important to bring the questions out of fearful hiding and to face them seriously, thoughtfully, together. The old tales offer a way which is direct, but without the pain of a personal experience. Here is a way which may in fact be a preparation for dealing later with the experiences that come—as they will—to everyone.

The hope is that discussion of the stories in this book may be helpful in developing positive beliefs which will create wider sympathies, greater confidence in life, a universality of approach to other people and other times, the opening of vistas for exploration, and the enriching of personal worth, ever growing with the upward thrust of life.

If, at the end of a story time, you should be the fortunate parent or teacher who will hear a child say, as Svetakata said to his father: "Please make me to understand more!" you may say to that child, "It shall be so. You shall learn more some other time!"

A GUIDE TO PRONUNCIATION

ā—as in *mate*
ä—as in *star*
ȧ—as in *task*
a̱—as in *hat*
ī—as in *mine*
i—as in *sin*
g—as in *good*

ē—as in *me*
e—as in *get*
ō—as in *note*
o—as in *not*
o͞o—as in *moon*
u—as in *but*
ụ—as in *push*

aborigines — a̱-bō-ri-jí-nēs
Admala — äd-mä́-lä
Alika — ä-le-kä
Ahura Mazda — ä-ho͞o-rä mäź-dä
Angri Manyi — äń-grē mäń-yē
Arjuna — äŕ-jụ-nä
at-man — ät́-mun
Bactria — bäk-trḗ-ä
Badahwedgi — bä-dä-wḗ-jē
Bakongo — bä-käń-gō
Benin — be-nīń
Bhagavadgita — bä-gä-väd-gḗ-tu
Brahman — brä́-mun
Capilanos — kä-pi-lä́-nōs
Choonhyang — cho͞on-yänǵ
Comanches — kō-man-ches
Dahomey — dä-hṓ-mē
dharma — däŕ-mä
Deucalion — do͞o-kä́-lē-on
Dritarashtra — dri-tä-räsh́-trȧ
Drapaudi — drä-poẃ-dē
duiker — dī́-ker
Dwaipayana Vyasa — dwī-pä-yä́-nä ve-ä́-sä
Duryodhana — do͞or-yō-dä́-nä

Ghasata	gä-sä‑tä
Gilgamesh	gil‑gu-mesh
Glooskap	gloōs-káp
Hermes	huŕ-mēs
Ilocanos	i-lō-kä‑nōs
Iroquois	iŕ-ä-kwoi
kashim	kä‑shēm
Kessapa	ke-sä‑på
Kalevala	kä-lä-vä-lä
Krishna	krish‑nä
kereru	ke‑re-roō
Kurukshetra	ku̧-ru̧k-shā‑trä
Lamang	lä‑mäng
Lu Sheng	loō-shung´
Mabouya	mä-boō-yä
Mahabharata	mä-häb-hä‑rä-tä
Maui	mow´-ē
Mawu	mä´-woō
Mondamin	mōn-dä‑min
Mpobe	Em‑pō-bē
Mt. Meru	mā‑rū
Nagasena	nä-gä-sā‑nȧ
Navajo	nä‑vä-hō
Nchonzo	chōn‑zō
Neamlau	nā-äm‑lōw
Nekumonta	ne-koō-mōn‑tä
Nurnderi	noō-run-dé‑rē
Nzambi Mpungu	zäm‑bē pun‑goō
Niyak	nē‑yäk
Pandava	pän-dä‑vä
Penobscots	pȩ-näb‑skäts
Pyrrha	pi‑rä
Shanewis	shä‑nu-wis
Svetakatu	své‑tä-kä-toō
Tambahillar	täm-bä-hí‑lur

Tao	tä-ō
Taranga	tä-rän-gu
Tyee	ti-ē
Ti Tuan	tē twän
Umuk	ōō-muk
Upanishads	U-pä-ni-shäds
Vainamoinen	vi-nä-moi-nen
Walumbe	wä-lum-bē
Wasis	wä-sis
Watadin	wä-tä-din
Yi Doryung	yē dōr-yung
Yang-yin	yäng-yēn
Yudisthira	ū-dis-thē-ra
Zeus	zōōs
Zoroaster	zō-rō-äs-ter